STAGING DARIO FO AND FRANCA RAME

Warwick Studies in the Humanities

The Humanities Research Centre of the University of Warwick in collaboration with Ashgate has re-launched its book series. Warwick Studies in the Humanities aims to bring together innovative work of a high academic standard which crosses disciplinary borders in the Arts and Humanities. It provides a forum for volumes exploring new dimensions of cultural history from the early modern period to the present, and for works that investigate aspects of contemporary cultural production within and across national boundaries. The series reflects the breadth of the interdisciplinary work carried out at Warwick's Humanities Research Centre, and includes work of both European and extra-European scope.

Series Editors

Dr Samantha Haigh (French Studies)
Dr Karen O'Brien (English & Comparative Literature)
Dr Loredana Polezzi (Italian Studies)

Series Advisory Board

Professor Susan Bassnett (Warwick)
Dr David Bradshaw (Worcester College, Oxford)
Professor Chris Clark (Warwick)
Professor Stuart Clark (Swansea)
Professor Richard Dyer (Warwick)
Professor Jo Labanyi (Institute of Romance Studies, London)
Professor Carolyn Steedman (Warwick)

Staging Dario Fo and Franca Rame

Anglo-American Approaches to Political Theatre

Stefania Taviano
University of Messina, Italy

ASHGATE

Published by
Ashgate Publishing Limited
Gower House
Croft Road
Aldershot
Hants GU11 3HR
England

Ashgate Publishing Company
Suite 420
101 Cherry Street
Burlington
Vermont, 05401–4405
USA

Ashgate website: http://www.ashgate.com

British Library Cataloguing in Publication Data
Taviano, Stefania
    Staging Dario Fo and Franca Rame: Anglo-American Approaches to Political Theatre. – (Warwick Studies in the Humanities)
    1. Fo, Dario – Stage history. 2. Fo, Dario – Criticism and interpretation. 3. Rame, Franca – Stage history. 4. Rame, Franca – Criticism and interpretation. 5. Theater – Italy – History – 20th century. 6. Theater – Political aspects. I. Title.
    852.9'14

US Library of Congress Cataloging in Publication Data
Taviano, Stefania
    Staging Dario Fo and Franca Rame: Anglo-American Approaches to Political Theatre / Stefania Taviano.
        p.   cm. – (Warwick Studies in the Humanities)
    Includes bibliographical references and index.
    1. Fo, Dario – Stage history. 2. Fo, Dario – Criticism and interpretation. 3. Rame, Franca – Stage history. 4. Rame, Franca – Criticism and interpretation. 5. Theater – Italy – History – 20th century. 6. Theater – Political aspects I. Title. II. Series.
    PQ4866.O2Z87 2006
    852'.914–dc22   2005013072

ISBN 0 7546 5401 X

free paper.
ain by MPG Books Ltd, Bodmin, Cornwall

Contents

List of Figures

Acknowledgments

I am particularly grateful to Franca Rame and Dario Fo for introducing me to their inspiring work, for being supportive of my research and for always being available to provide all the material and information I needed.

I acknowledge a special debt of gratitude to Susan Bassnett, who has always been a guide for me and who has believed in my work since when I was a graduate student; to Loredana Polezzi for her encouragement and for always being ready to offer invaluable criticism throughout the making of this book; to Maria Panarello for her scrupolous help and unfailing support.

I wish to thank Ann Donahue, my commissioning editor for believing in this book before it took shape. My gratitude to Tony Howard, Ron Jenkins, Tony Mitchell, Ed Emery, Tom Behan, Joseph Farrell, Jennifer Lorch, Ron Davis, Walter Valeri, Christopher Cairns, Joan Holden, Geoff Hoyle, Gillian Hanna, Richard Seyd, Tony Taccone, Richard Hamburger, Norma Saldivar and Joe Hanreddy for answering my questions and for providing me with valuable material. Thank you also to Simon Tanner for reading my work.

I would also like to acknowledge the help of Marina de Juli, Marco Scordo and Eliel Ferreira, when consulting Fo and Rame's archives; and of the staff of the Royal National Theatre archives, of the Theatre Museum and of the New York Public Library for their kindness and help.

Thanks are due to Emma McKee, Tim Peterson, Amy Lacy, Allen Nomura, Kati Mitchell, Bob Aird, Linda Blasé, Richard Feldman, Lex Leifheit, Bill Burkhart, Nick Lacy and Simon Warner for providing me with photographs of productions. Thanks also to Maria Ficara, Mariavita Cambria, Vincenza Minutella, Joy Sisley, Taira Savio, Charlotte Ross and Julie Gilson for their true friendship and support.

Finally I am happy to express my warmest thanks to my family, and above all to my mother, for being the first to have faith in my work.

To my partner Elshafie E. M. Idriss for being by my side and, most of all, for believing in me, thank you.

Sections of chapter one originally appeared in 'Italian culture on the American stage', *Journal of Literature and Aesthetics*, vol. 8, no. 2, July - December 2000, pp. 90-102. Sections of chapter three originally appeared in 'Dario Fo and Franca Rame in the United Kingdom', in Edward M. Batley and David Bradby (eds) *Morality and Justice - The Challenge of European Theatre*. Amsterdam: Rodopi, 2001, pp. 285-298.

Introduction

This book focuses on the translation and stage production of Dario Fo and Franca Rame's theatre in two English-speaking countries, the United Kingdom and the United States, seen in the broader context of these countries' attitudes towards foreign cultures and theatres. In looking at the ways in which Fo and Rame's plays are received by English-speaking cultures, this book fills a gap by providing an extensive analysis of the reputation of Fo and Rame in two countries outside Italy. It also contributes to the study of theatre as a central practice in intercultural relations. Given that the way in which political theatre is translated and received depends on the cultural, sociopolitical and theatrical makeup of the target society, there are no general patterns that are valid for the translation and staging of Fo and Rame's political theatre in any culture. Their work is instead subject to specific strategies and traditions, which are the product of the cultural and theatrical systems of the receiving societies and of the interaction between the latter and foreign cultures. It is by addressing the problematic issue of what constitutes political theatre in a given society that it becomes clear how such a definition can be used as a handy label, a category to identify theatre texts that are disturbing, challenging and therefore difficult to stage.

In the past few years Fo and Rame's theatre has been subject to a renewed critical interest aimed at a full revaluation by devoting attention to previously neglected aspects of their work. Among others, a monograph has been devoted to the often underestimated role of Rame, *Franca Rame. A Woman on Stage* (2000). Joseph Farrell and Antonio Scuderi's, *Dario Fo: Stage, Text and Tradition* (2001) offers a re-examination of Fo's work, from an historical perspective, aimed at identifying Fo's poetics and the contradictions between his radical political views and his rather conservative theatrical credo. At the same time, as Farrell argues in the first full biography of Fo and Rame in English (2001), given the international interest in their theatre there are innumerable productions of their plays around the world. As a result, there is an overwhelming quantity of material which needs to be studied and which cannot be covered in a single work. This explains the precise focus of this book, which aims to examine the approach of the United Kingdom and the United States towards Fo and Rame's theatre by considering two main points.

First, the unique nature of Fo and Rame's work, due to its immediacy in social and political terms, which makes the study of its transposition to English-speaking societies a fascinating case study. The essence of Fo and Rame's political theatre lies in a multifaceted notion of struggle, as emerged from my recent interview with Rame for the ninth issue of the international theatre journal *Open Page* focusing on 'theatre, women and struggle'. As a woman for whom struggle is a raison d'être, as writer, actress, wife of the Nobel Prize winner Fo, Rame was asked to discuss her commitment to struggle in its many connotations. Struggle intended as a political struggle, a class struggle, a social struggle, a struggle for the weakest. Rame and Fo's theatre in fact cannot be separated from their commitment to social, cultural and political issues, which has marked their private and public lives and makes it unique.

Second, the fact that foreign political theatre undergoes a significant process of manipulation when translated into English, as is emphasised by critics and scholars who often talk of their 'misconception' or 'distortion'. More precisely, it is the combination of such a complex phenomenon as Fo and Rame's theatre with the influence of the target cultural and theatrical systems which determine an intricate process of appropriation. This book addresses such key issues by examining the cultural and theatrical factors affecting the selection and transformation of Fo and Rame's political plays in both British and American cultures. It aims to show that their theatre was successfully staged thanks to a process of commercialisation opposed to the revolutionary nature of their work.

The process of transferring Fo and Rame's plays to British and American cultures does not simply involve the translation of the *dramatic text*, defined by Patrice Pavis as 'the verbal script which is read or heard in performance'. (Pavis, 1992: 24) The dramatic text is only one element in a multilevel combination of different signifying systems. Rather than focusing on the translated dramatic text, i.e. the literary script, this book looks at all the different elements of stage productions of Fo and Rame's plays resulting in the *mise en scène*. Scholars such as Tadeusz Kowzan (1974), Marco de Marinis (1982), Keir Elam (1980), Erika Fischer-Lichte (1984) have emphasised the importance of the performance as a 'text'. The notion of 'testo spettacolare', the performance text or spectacle text, as it has been variously defined, testifies to what Pavis has identified as 'a desire to get away from a logocentric notion of theatre with the text as the central and stable element.' (Pavis, 1992: 32). Pavis's definition of performance text as 'the *mise en scène* of a reading and any possible account made of this reading by a spectator' appears to be one of the most fruitful. This book will in fact be focusing not only on the *mise en scène*, as single instances of British and American stage rewriting of Fo and Rame's plays, but also on the overall 'stage interpretation' of their theatre (Pavis, 1982: 160). In other words, this analysis of the translation of Fo and Rame's political theatre in English-speaking countries seeks to look at the ways in which their plays are interpreted not only by translators, but also by theatre practitioners, such as actors and directors, when they are put on stage for local audiences in the receiving society.

As Marvin Carlson argues:

the performance does not come into our culture like a painting, as an external object to be understood, but if it is to exist for us at all must be created again, from within our culture and using the tools of our own culture, with correspondingly far greater risk that the product will in fact ultimately be a reflection of our culture rather than of its own. (Carlson, 1990: 118)

In this book I intend to examine predominant patterns of appropriation of Fo and Rame's plays in British and American cultures, going from the way their dramatic texts are translated into English to the theatrical traditions affecting the *mise en scène* of their plays. This is why **chapter one**, in particular, looks at the overall question of reception by taking into account the impact that the theatrical system and cultural system of the target societies have on the productions of Fo and Rame's plays. The practice of adapting their plays on the basis of 'literal' translations, the acting styles adopted in staging their theatre, the stage representation of images of Italian culture are some of the main aspects analysed in the first chapter. They constitute an integral part of the overall process of rewriting of Fo and Rame's plays to make them fit into the British and American repertoire of theatre texts. In this sense it can be argued that productions of Fo and Rame's plays, together with those of other foreign plays, represent a subcategory within the domestic theatre system.

Moreover, Fo and Rame's plays belong to a particular group within that subcategory, that is to say *political theatre*. Political theatre is commonly associated with left-wing theatre. However, current theatre scholarship and practices clearly show that any attempt to discuss the meaning and significance of political theatre today needs to start from an awareness that this category has become highly problematic and open to question. A number of scholars, such as Eugène Van Erven (1988), Baz Kershaw (1992), Graham Holderness (1992), have shown precisely how difficult it is to identify political theatre as a well defined category. This is due to the incredibly wide range of theatrical events and activities which constitute political theatre in different ways and to different extents. Jeanne Colleran and Jenny Spencer (1998) introduce their book on political theatre by emphasizing the ambiguous nature and vulnerability of both political theatre and criticism of it, as well as indicating the editors' and contributors' common belief in the capacity of theatre to promote social transformation. **Chapter two** therefore starts by addressing the problematic issues of what constitutes political theatre and then examines the peculiarities of Fo and Rame's revolutionary theatre within the Italian political context. The challenges and obstacles set by a number of Fo and Rame's untranslated political plays will be looked at to show how their didactic nature has prevented them from being appealing to foreign audiences. Furthermore, a brief analysis of English-language stagings of Bertolt Brecht's theatre will allow the identification of some of the main strategies and tendencies of British and American theatre systems towards foreign political plays.

This will be followed by a detailed history of British translations and stagings of Fo and Rame's plays in **chapter three**. When it comes to the interpretation and reproduction of Fo and Rame's plays in English, the significance of their political theatre depends even more on the cultural and historical perspectives that are being considered. In other words, we need to take into account two different perspectives at the same time: the meaning and role of political theatre in the source culture on the one hand and the significance of political theatre in the target theatrical and cultural system. This is why chapter three starts by looking at British political theatre groups before moving to the main aspects of British stagings of Fo and Rame's work. When Fo and Rame's work is staged in the United Kingdom, the theatrical quality of their plays is given priority over their political role and they are reduced to plays with only a political content, if that, in order to make them fit in with British theatre practices. Thanks to a process of anglicisation of their work, Fo and Rame became incredibly successful in the 1980s in the United Kingdom. It will be shown how, despite the political commitment of theatre groups such as Belt and Braces, the target theatrical and cultural constraints created a predominantly comic interpretation of their plays at the expense of their political function.

Chapter four focuses on the Americanisation of Fo and Rame's theatre which reveals similar aspects to the British approach, such as the tendency to highlight the comic aspects of their theatre. As in chapter three, the nature of political theatre and actor training in the United States will be examined to show how it has affected American *mises en scène* of Fo and Rame's work. Among other things, the fiasco of the Broadway production of *Accidental Death of an Anarchist* (*Morte accidentale di un anarchico*) represents a unique example of the impact of target theatrical and cultural constraints on the reception of Fo and Rame's theatre. The denial of an American visa to Fo and Rame three times is another aspect of the history of Fo and Rame's theatre in the United States which is also taken into account. The final part of the chapter looks at productions which represent an alternative to the predominant process of Americanisation to which Fo and Rame's plays are subject.

Chapter five investigates the meaning of Fo and Rame's political theatre today and looks at contemporary approaches to their theatre. In 1996 Baz Kershaw rightly argued that performance practices aimed at being oppositional have lost their value. This is due to a number of reasons such as the collapse of Communism and the lack of confidence in the legitimacy of political practices characteristic of contemporary capitalist democracies. Furthermore, because of the mediatisation and globalisation of our society, 'the ideological functions of performance become ever more diverse, and perhaps, diluted' and it is no longer valid to talk about political theatre as a separate category (Kershaw, 1996: 133). In Kershaw's view we can only distinguish between more or less politically effective kinds of performance. Four productions are analysed in this chapter: the 2003 Scottish staging of *Mistero Buffo* and the same year West End production of *Accidental Death of an Anarchist*, the 2001 American première of *Johan Padan and the Discovery of the Americas* (*Johan Padan a la descoverta de le Americhe*) and the 2004 staging of Ron Jenkins's new translation of *Accidental Death of an Anarchist*. These productions indicate the coexistence of traditional translation strategies with new approaches to Fo and Rame's theatre.

The concluding chapter considers the fact that Fo and Rame's most recent plays are practically ignored in the United Kingdom, whereas hits such as *Accidental Death of an Anarchist* continue to be staged in the London West End. This means that, on the one hand, recent British productions of Fo and Rame's classics reflect a dominant strategy adopted in stagings of foreign playwrights. On the other hand, Jenkins's translations indicate the possibility of a new approach to foreign theatre. Such an approach reflects Hal Foster's argument for postmodern art to be resistant rather than transgressive given that the postmodern artist can only operate within the culture he/she criticises (Foster, 1985). It will be argued that appropriate acting techniques and an innovative use of theatrical spaces are some of the main aspects of a resistant response to foreign plays that does not focus on their cultural origins.

While this book shows that fundamental aspects of stage representations and theatre practices have been transmitted from one generation to the next and continue to affect stagings of Fo and Rame's plays, it also demonstrates that theatrical traditions evolve and change in time according to social and historical conditions. The history of British and American stagings of Fo and Rame's plays tells us a great deal about the cultural dynamics of the receiving societies through the ways in which images of the Other and the Self are negotiated on the stage. If Fo and Rame's theatre constitutes a space for social critique and debate, the analysis of the rewriting of their plays acquires a huge significance in revealing the social and cultural practices that govern relations between different cultures. This book opens the way for future critical studies that will investigate further the politics behind the translation and stage production of political theatre in a number of cultures.

Chapter 1

Transposing Theatre across Cultures

When foreign plays are transposed into English, they are incorporated in the repertoire of theatre texts of the receiving society. Hence they go through an elaborate process of adjustment, made up of different phases. Each phase corresponds to the interpretation of theatre practitioners whose task is to make the foreign text familiar and acceptable to the target audience. It will be helpful in this first chapter to investigate some general patterns inherent to the process of translation of foreign plays to show how they apply to and affect the British and American approach to Fo and Rame's theatre. Such introductory analysis will provide us with an overall picture of predominant theatre and cultural practices before going into a detailed study of British and American productions of their plays. More precisely, the use of 'literal' translations of Fo and Rame's plays, the acting styles adopted in the productions and the stage representations of Italian culture are predominant factors shaping the process of appropriation of Fo and Rame's plays. These factors will be considered within the overall question of the reception of Fo and Rame's plays, affected by the British and American tendency to rewrite the otherness of foreign cultures.

Translation does not take place in isolation. It is the result of social, cultural and economic constraints which shape the coming into existence of the foreign text. When foreign plays are translated into English, the British and American theatrical systems have an enormous impact on the way their plays are interpreted. The target theatrical system consists of a combination of all those theatrical factors shaping the *mise en scène*. The theatrical system of a society includes predominant acting styles, domestic traditions in terms of specific theatrical genres and subsequent audience expectations. Also relevant are the agenda of the theatre(s) staging the *mise en scène*, combined with the audience's preference and familiarity with a specific repertoire, the policy of cultural institutions, such as public bodies controlling the allocation of funding to the arts.[1] All of these factors are then informed by the social, cultural and historical framework surrounding them. The theatrical system shaping translation discourse is strictly linked to the values of the society to which it belongs. The way in which foreign plays are performed and interpreted is affected by cultural codes and values governing society at large.

An element of the target theatrical system which shapes the translation of plays into English is the practice of so-called 'literal translations'. Commissioning

---

[1] Theatrical system is the term that Sirkuu Aaltonen similarly uses to refer to the network of producer and consumer subsystems shaping the translation of theatre texts. Aaltonen (2000).

'literal translations', which supposedly provide an 'accurate' rendering of the foreign text, later adapted by theatre practitioners, represents a British and American policy often adopted in the translation of foreign theatre texts. The assumption that a literal translation provides an accurate rendering of the foreign text is a claim used to minimise the arbitrary nature of this practice. One only needs to consider the notion which supposedly justifies the use of literal translations and their subsequent adaptation by dramatists, i.e. the speakability of the translated text. Since it is commonly argued that the translation of a play needs to be speakable, that its dialogue needs to be fluent, a theatre professional, such as a director or a dramatist, is the only person considered to be capable of performing such a task, whereas it is believed that translators are not in the position to produce a speakable text. Such strategy reflects the negative implications that copyright law has on the status and financial rewards of the translator in theatre. What this practice involves in real terms is paying a very low fee to an unknown translator, in several cases without even acknowledging his/her work, to produce a text which will then be made 'speakable' or 'performable' by a well known playwright or director. The latter's name in the promotional material and in the theatre programme ensures, or at least contributes to, the success of the stage production. In most instances those who are recognised as adaptors do not know the source language.

Most stagings of Fo and Rame's texts in English are based on a literal translation used as the starting point of a so-called 'adaptation'. The first major British production of *Accidental Death of an Anarchist*, staged in 1979 by the socialist company Belt and Braces, was directed and adapted by Gavin Richards from a literal translation by Gillian Hanna. Although Hanna's name appears in the programme, Gavin Richards is the one who has been given all the credit and who has mainly benefited financially from the enormous success of that production.[2] As will be shown in chapter three, Richards's adaptation presented British audiences with a very different play from the one known by Italian audiences on a number of levels, from the alterations of the dramatic text to the theatrical style adopted for the *mise en scène*. The second main staging of *Accidental Death of an Anarchist* took place in January 1991 at the National Theatre and the translated text was identified as 'a new English version' by Alan Cumming and Tim Supple. This more recent text was defined as a new English version simply to distinguish it from the first one and to identify it as a text closer to the 'spirit' of the original. When the second production came out it was emphasised that, while the first focused on a comic interpretation of the play, as Fo complained (quoted in Nightingale, 1991: 14), affecting the political content of the source text, this 'new version' was based on a British approach, in Cumming's view (quoted in Kaye, 1991: 17), and enriched with references to British political events. The question is then, in what

---

[2] When I interviewed her in 1998 Gillian Hanna explained that Gavin Richards exploited her since she was given practically nothing compared to the huge earnings derived from the success of that and successive productions.

way is the 'new English version' different from the previous 'adaptation'? And on what grounds do we distinguish between an 'adaptation' and 'a new version'? As will be shown in chapter three, they both alter the source text in different ways, the first to make it funnier and fit it into the English tradition of the music-hall and the second to make it more relevant to the experience of target spectators.

There are also more complex cases which show how the multiple interpretation process of theatre texts is made up of a number of layers, all connected to each other, some of which are more visible than others. The American première of Dario Fo's *We Can't Pay? We Won't Pay!* (*Non si paga! Non si paga!*) in 1979, presented by the San Francisco Mime Troupe, was based on a British translation by Lino Pertile, which was adapted by Bill Colvill and Robert Walker, and an American translation by the People's Translation Service and the San Francisco Mime Troupe, which was adapted by the San Francisco Mime Troupe itself. Here we have a text, which is the result of two translations, a British one and a collective American one, as in the tradition of the San Francisco Mime Troupe, both of which are then further adapted. The Mime Troupe calls this a 'version', just like the above-mentioned English text of *Accidental Death of an Anarchist* by Cumming and Supple: 'Fo wanted us not to use the translation from the London production. Along with Joan Holden and the People's Translation Service, we have been working on a more idiomatic, American version, which we think he'll like' (quoted in Weiner, 1979: 22). And this is the comment of a critic: 'There are a few references in the script that might be considered too typically Italian, but the version presented here ably makes the transition to the American idiom.' (Weiner, 1979: 12) The 'version' is praised by the reviewer because it sounds American enough, although we are reminded that it still contains aspects which appear excessively Italian from an American perspective.

The multiple translation of *We Can't Pay? We Won't Pay!*, the combination of a British text with an American one, as well as being Fo's request, has to do with the target theatrical system and with the tendency to adapt texts written in British English to ensure that they appear and sound American to local audiences. British adaptations are not well perceived by American critics and directors due to the differences between British and American English. This is the view of Norma Saldivar, director for the Milwaukee Repertory Theatre and Madison Civic Center, who directed a student production of Ron Davis's translation, entitled *We Won't Pay! We Won't Pay!*, at the University of Wisconsin, Madison in 1998. She argues that more often than not American directors are forced to use British translations of foreign plays simply because American translations are not available.[3] Hence they find themselves dealing with texts that linguistically do not work on the American stage because British English often sounds awkward, and in some cases funny to American ears. Such an approach towards British translations is confirmed by the fiasco of the American première of Eduardo De Filippo's *Filumena Marturano*,

---

[3] Interview with Norma Saldivar, Madison, Wisconsin, June 2000.

based on an English version by Keith Waterhouse and Willis Hall.[4] The production was badly received and one of the aspects of the show held responsible for its failure was the British English of the translation. Critics' comments indicated that the language of Hall and Waterhouse's adaptation had not been Americanised and their negative reaction to the use of British terms showed that the language of the adaptation affected, to a certain extent, American responses to the play.[5]

Needless to say, linguistic divergencies represent one among a number of obstacles for a British translation to be staged in the United States, although it might be the most obvious and more easily perceived by audiences and critics. Among other things, a British translation bears the weight of cultural and above all political differences between the two countries which inevitably affect its transposition on the American stage. When staged in the United States it might lose its efficacy and relevance because some of its cultural and political references are lost on American audiences or because those references acquire a different value affecting the reception of a play. Particularly in the case of Fo and Rame's theatre since translators and theatre practitioners, in their attempt to reproduce the political function of their plays, need to insert references to political and social issues of the receiving society. One of the consequences of such obstacles is that directors have to adapt the translation to an American context and therefore productions of foreign plays in the United States can often be based on translations of translations, as in the above-mentioned example of *We Can't Pay? We Won't Pay!*. This means that extra layers of interpretation are added to the already complex process of translation, but without being based on the source text.

Furthermore, the vagueness of the terms adopted to define translations of Fo and Rame's theatre texts is determined by the peculiarity of theatre practices and can be explained to a certain extent as a result of the tendency to justify a free approach to foreign texts, which seems to be tolerated more easily in translation of plays. A translation of a novel, which cuts out large passages of the source text, moves others and makes the language much more vulgar, as in the case of Gavin Richards's version of *Accidental Death of an Anarchist*, would probably not be as easily accepted as a translation of that particular novel by that particular author. Marvin Carlson, commenting on the attitude of Samuel Beckett and Arthur Miller, who took legal action against companies which modified their texts, states that all such efforts at controlling the libidinal flow of performance have failed, leaving intact a more basic tradition according to which dramatic scripts have always been cut, elaborated, or modified according to these exigencies of the performance situation (Carlson, 1999: 115). The range of such exigencies is incredibly vast. It can go from the need to adapt the linguistic medium of the foreign text to the limits imposed by the cast of the theatre company performing the play, to the physical

[4] The production was first staged at the Shubert Theatre, in Boston, in December 1979, it was directed by Franco Zeffirelli and starred Joan Plowright, Frank Finlay and Ernest Sarracino.
[5] See Warren, 1980; Simon, 1980.

constraints of the stage, and so on. Moreover one cannot deny that the ephemeral nature of theatre, and in particular of the language of theatre texts, which needs to be altered to travel not only between cultures, but also within the same society from one period to another, appear to justify their continuous rewriting. Hence interpreters of Fo and Rame's plays tend to base the legitimacy of their reading on the necessity to update theatre texts according to new audiences and new contexts of performance.

However, even before they are transposed to foreign cultures, Fo and Rame's theatre texts are constantly modified according to audience reactions and the political events that they document. There are several versions of most of their plays and this complicates even further the process of translation and production of their work outside Italy. For example, when Mitchell translated *Mum's Marijuana is the Best (La marijuana della mamma è la più bella)*, he was asked to work from a tape recording of Fo and Rame's most recent performance because it represented the most up-to-date version of the play (Mitchell, 1999). During Fo and Rame's visit to the United States in October 2000, Rame performed *Sesso, grazie tanto per gradire* in Italian with English surtitles based on Jenkins's translation, *Sex? Thanks, Don't Mind if I Do!* Jenkins's translation, which was only a few months old, needed to be updated since it included parts of the monologue that Rame had already cut in her constant editing of the text (Jenkins, 2000).

Ed Emery's commitment to Fo and Rame's theatre and his translations represent an exception to the above-mentioned practice of adapting their plays. He explains on his web site devoted to Fo and Rame that 'In translating these plays, I do not usually adapt them. I seek to stay as close as possible to the original Italian, while at the same time creating good performance pieces.'[6] He has translated several plays, some of which have been published: *Accidental Death of an Anarchist* (1992), *Mistero Buffo* (1988) and *One was Nude and One Wore Tails* (1992) by Methuen; *The Pope and the Witch* and *The First Miracle of the Boy Jesus* by Oberon (1994). His aim is to make all his unpublished translations available as part of his archive and to provide 'complete performance texts on-line.' Emery has received the same treatment as other translators who have provided literal translations of Fo and Rame's plays. His translation of *The Pope and the Witch*, analysed in chapter three, was adapted by Andy de la Tour, who does not speak Italian. The production was first staged at the West Yorkshire Playhouse and then moved to London in 1992. Emery demanded a higher percentage of royalties for the London production, which was denied him. Furthermore, as Emery explained when I interviewed him in 1998, the problem with that translation was that by mistake he had been given an earlier version of the play rather than the one published by Einaudi. This created misunderstandings and Fo and Rame criticised his translation.

---

[6] See www.emery.archive.mcmail.com.

The cases analysed so far are examples of how the translation of the dramatic text is influenced by target theatrical systems and they show the complex mechanisms of interpretation to which Fo and Rame's plays are subject starting from the written text. But we have only begun to unfold one among several components of the overall performance text, which is even more clearly shaped by theatrical traditions and acting styles. For example, one aspect of the British, as well as American, theatrical system representing an obstacle to the stagings of Fo and Rame's work is actor training, which is radically different from the kind of training predominant in Italy. One major problem for English-speaking actors is that of conveying physical rhythms when performing Fo and Rame's plays. The principles on which Fo and Rame's theatre is founded are exactly the opposite of those informing the Stanislavskyan approach, which gives priority to an actor's psychological interpretation of a character. When Fo and Rame's plays are staged in the United Kingdom and the United States actors and directors tend to interpret them from a naturalistic perspective. This is a central issue which largely affects the staging and therefore the reception of Fo and Rame's theatre, as will be further shown. According to Saldivar (2000), given the strong influence of realism in American acting training, actors tend to shy from political theatre because they do not want to be a vehicle for political ideas and ideals. She argues that American actors are too accustomed to psychological interpretation to perform in a play which, in their view and experience, is didactic and does not allow them to develop their interpretation in realistic terms. This means that it might be difficult to find American actors willing to interpret Fo and Rame's work and with the adequate training to do so.

At the same time, there has been a tendency, in a number of cases, to accentuate the intensity of speeches and dialogues in Fo and Rame's plays, to emphasise the exuberance of the Latin temperament of the characters. This is the result produced on stage of a cultural framework, i.e. the Anglo-American interpretation of Italian culture. In other words, it is the theatrical reflection, the visual rendering of the way Italians are perceived in British and American society. As Fo argues, caricatured images of Italians are widespread: 'Everywhere I go I see Italians with moustaches and sideburns, rings on their fingers and white shoes. It's as though all English plays were performed by men in bowler hats' (quoted in Edwardes, 1992). This is one of the main aspects of what I call *stage representations of immigrants*, i.e. theatrical interpretations of foreign cultures in English-speaking cultures, a point to which I will come back later.

Acting style on the one hand, and cultural images on the other, or better the combination of both, largely affect the transposition of Fo and Rame's plays into English. In this sense, British and American stagings of their theatre testify to the interrelation between the theatrical system and the cultural system of reference. In 1999 two productions of *We Won't Pay! We Won't Pay!* were staged in the United States. One at the Trinity Repertory Theatre, in Providence, based on the 'North American version' by Davis, directed by Amanda Denhert. The setting of the production looked like an Italian Street Festival. Patrons were directed to follow red, white or green lights, depending on their assigned seats. A bar was part of the set and the audience was encouraged to arrive half an hour early to purchase Italian food and drinks from street vendors put on different levels and to sit at café tables, while being entertained by street musicians Kevin Fallon, Rachel Maloney and Chris Turner. The set was complete with clotheslines with laundry and Soviet and Italian flags. On stage right there was a 20-foot neon-blue Pope with a door through his robes that lit up whenever his name was invoked. At the opening the characters sang the famous Italian American song *Santa Lucia*, one of them introduced himself as 'Sal Monella' and asked the audience: 'Is that big enough-a Pope or what?' The show surrounding the show, i.e. the performance of *We Won't Pay! We Won't Pay!*, and the introduction of Italian American music are clearly theatrical choices, though at the same time strictly related to the cultural context surrounding them. The staging strategy adopted in this production is related to popular American shows about Italian culture, such as *Tony and Tina's Wedding*, an interactive show staged in a New York Italian restaurant, where spectators eat Italian food while assisting and being involved in an Italian style wedding. [7]

The other 1999 production of *We Won't Pay! We Won't Pay!* was staged at the American Repertory Theatre, in a translation by Ron Jenkins, and was presented to the audience within 'a cabaret frame'. When the spectators came into the foyer, they were welcomed by the actor playing Giovanni, who was singing songs such as *That's Amore* and *Santa Lucia* on a stage dominated by a revolving Tower of Pisa. At the end of the show, all the actors were dancing and singing the same songs in a *Saturday Night Fever* style. These were specific choices of the director and the actor playing Giovanni who, having recently performed in a cabaret piece, suggested the idea of interacting with the audience by singing. Such choices not only had not been predetermined by the translation, but they were in conflict with the approach of the translator and Fo himself, who condemned them and tried to have them eliminated from the production without success. The introduction of Italian American songs in both productions, the use of larger than life props representing symbols of Italian culture, the Pope and the Tower of Pisa, the superficial cultural jokes, all testify to the impact that cultural images combined with theatrical traditions have on the way Fo and Rame's plays are staged and therefore perceived by English-speaking audiences. The extent to which the choices made by the directors and the other interpreters of the text affected the target culture's perception of *We Won't Pay! We Won't Pay!* is evident in the kind of publicity that some critics gave to the play. James Merolla wrote in the *Sun Chronicle*:

---

[7] The show has been playing since 6 February 1988. The religious ceremony is staged at St Luke's Church and is followed by a reception at the Vinnie Black's Coliseum at the Edison Hotel, Manhattan. According to the official *Tony and Tina's wedding* web site, this is 'the second largest running show in Off-Broadway and the longest running comedy ever'. www.tonylovestina.com

Do yourself a favor. Don't dwell on the Socialist bent that Fo professed in the mid-70s about workers uniting against "big bosses" and overthrowing the right wingers. Instead, sit back and revel in the delicious performances given by the small, brilliant cast of five veteran Trinity actors. (...) There is a better kind of Marxism here. Groucho Marxism. And it is almost un-American not to laugh at this wonderful brand of slap-stick. (Merolla, 1999: 17)

Together with the previously mentioned productions of *We Won't Pay! We Won't Pay!*, many others which will be analysed further on indicate that the reception of Fo and Rame's plays, as in the case of any foreign play, can never take place without being somehow affected by the British and American images of Italian cultures. As Erika Fischer-Lichte argues, meaning in a text is created by means of internal and external decoding, the latter being strictly related to cultural knowledge, and to specific categories of knowledge: 'Such stocks of knowledge include all forms of cultural stereotypes such as the image of a king wearing a crown; an Indian with a feather head-dress; and the stereotypes of the stiff Englishman, the thrifty Scotsman, the proud Spaniard, etc.' (Fischer-Lichte, 1984: 241). The stereotypes about a foreign culture, which are part of the broader image through which the otherness of that culture can be interpreted, function as fundamental extratheatrical elements to which textual elements can be related by the receiver. In the case of Fo and Rame's translated plays, the writers of target texts rely to various degrees on those common 'stocks of knowledge', such as stereotypes on Italian culture, to facilitate the understanding of the foreign text, to make it appear comfortably familiar. In this analysis stereotypes about foreign cultures are not primarily and solely considered as the product of negative perceptions about foreigners; rather, they are analysed in terms of their overall impact as culturally and socially transmitted set of beliefs on the relationship between English-speaking cultures and foreign cultures.

Such specialised knowledge contributes to create certain expectations in the spectators of any theatrical production. The role of the audience, together with that of the critics, as active agents in the reception of Fo and Rame's plays constitute a central aspect of the present analysis. As Hans Robert Jauss argues, for every work of art there is a certain disposition of the audience preceding the individual reaction and understanding of each member of the public, a disposition which arises in the historical moment of the appearance of a given work and which is determined by a combination of aesthetic and extratextual factors (Jauss, 1982: 23). What Jauss writes about the literary experience of a reader can be applied to the relation between the appearance of a theatre text, in this case of a foreign play, and its audience. But, as Susan Bennett emphasises, diverse horizons of expectations coexist within a given culture and they are not stable or fixed; on the contrary, they can be modified and renegotiated at any time (Bennett, 1990). In his metaphor of the hourglass of cultural exchange, Pavis also looks at the impact of the transcultural *mise en scène* on the target audience and defines this phase of the reception process as 'the given and anticipated consequences' (Pavis, 1992: 209).

Among a spectator's possible reactions to cultural otherness considered by Pavis, there is the tendency to reinforce his/her perception of the foreign culture or conversely to deny that image in order to create a new one.

This also applies to the production and reception of Fo and Rame's theatre in English-speaking countries. Stage representations of Italians belong to the horizon of expectations that American and British audiences bring to productions of Fo and Rame's plays, but each spectator will carry such expectations in varying degrees and to different extents. At the same time the performance text will challenge or reinforce those expectations in ways that will vary according to the individual experience of the spectator. The same holds true for critics: on the one hand there are those who condemn the use of stage representations of Italians as a theatrical framing, and on the other there are those who praise it for allowing a supposedly genuine presentation of the foreign culture.

In his seminal essay on signs of Italianness, where he analyses the linguistic message, the coded iconic message and the non-coded iconic message of the Panzani advertisement, Roland Barthes argues that the variety of readings of the same image depends on individuals, but that such variations are connected to the kind of knowledge applied to the image. In particular he refers to 'a body of attitudes' that individuals apply in their reading of an image, for example 'tourism', which varies from one person to another. Hence the importance of the two sides of the coin: the knowledge and attitude invested in the image by its producers, but also by its receivers. As Barthes puts it, 'the language of the image is not merely the totality of the utterances emitted, it is also the totality of utterances received' (Barthes, 1977: 47) and both aspects of the image of Italianness in English-speaking countries need to be taken into account. The American response to the Broadway production of *Accidental Death of an Anarchist* in 1984, which was a total fiasco, serves as a revealing case of the way in which the response of the critics as well as the target audience's horizon of expectations affect the success or failure of a show.[8]

In order to better understand the origins of stage representations of immigrants, we need to briefly look at nineteenth-century vaudeville. Vaudeville was a very popular form of entertainment, together with minstrel shows, at the turn of the twentieth century. From the late 1850s, following the first phase of immigration from Europe, the immigrants, with their foreign features, started to be represented on the American stage and became a new source of entertainment. While previously the Yankee or the Negro were portrayed on stage because they were different from Americans, now the immigrants were the ones who did not go unnoticed since they looked, behaved, dressed and spoke differently. A vaudeville actor simply needed to carefully watch a foreigner, focus on his/her most prominent exotic traits and then recreate them for American audiences. As Carl Wittke claims, 'In these stage presentations, however crude, exaggerated and

---

[8] See also Susan Bennett, *Theatre Audiences: A Theory of Production and Reception* (London and New York: Routledge, 1990).

untrue, we have the beginnings of certain realism in the American drama, for they were based on actual observation of life experiences' (Wittke, 1952: 212).

So-called racial or ethnic acts, vaudeville acts focusing on the immigrant experience of the Germans, the Irish, the Jews and the Italians, were created at the time of mass immigration and became extremely popular from the 1870s to the 1920s. The accent, the clothes and the facial features, including the colour of the skin – Irish skin was red while the Sicilian complexion was olive – were the most important factors through which the immigrants were identified. For example, the German or Dutch figure could be recognised because of his physical appearance and his clothes. Moreover, his limited knowledge of English and his accent made him appear as not a particularly intelligent character. In Claudia Orenstein's words:

> All popular forms rely on easily recognizable, stock characters appearing over and over again in different contexts. They embody simplified emotional and psychological traits and perform very clear actions. ... In their very simplicity, however, these characters also appeal to popular prejudices. The stereotypes prevalent in popular forms are almost always comic caricatures. (Orenstein, 1998: 93)

The accent convention, in other words the use of fake accents as a form of identification of specific stage characters, was one of the most recurring elements of ethnic acts. The Italians were known, among other things, for their thick accent. This was the time when the identifying traits of the Italian accent, which were also applied to Italian characters in American plays in the following century, were set, as testified to by a monologue written by William McNally for a vaudeville act entitled *My Big-a Brother Joe*, beginning with: 'My big-a brother he got-a the head like-a the macaroni' (McNally, 1919). These were the central aspects of the so-called Italian speech: the addition of the unstressed root vowel 'a' as in looka, finda, havea, tella, musta, killa, together with the replacement of 'th' at the beginning of words with 'd' and the omission of the final consonant or vowel in a word.

Vaudeville performers stressed the authenticity of the characters presented on stage. These stereotypes, which corresponded to everyday life people and developed with them, were a constant element in vaudeville acts and their popularity continued to grow. It was precisely the close relation between ethnic characters and the immigrants they caricatured which made them particularly attractive to American spectators. The realism, which continued to dominate American drama and affect productions of domestic and foreign plays, long before the Stanislavsky acting Method was imported in the thirties by the New York based Group Theatre, appears to have originated in historical and social conditions in nineteenth century America. Despite the fact that both minstrel shows and ethnic acts were the product of specific American social and historical circumstances, they were not limited to America. In fact the most famous and successful vaudeville performers travelled to Europe and were very successful on British music-hall stages. At the same time British music-hall and variety performers also toured in America, hence it can be said that there was a reciprocal influence between the two countries.

It will be shown how British and American directors and producers' concern to ensure that Fo and Rame's plays are funny and entertaining would appear to be the legacy of these historical representations of immigrants and related theatrical traditions. This is because stage representations of Italian culture continue, to a certain extent, to represent the interpretative frame through which British and American rewriters of Italian theatre present it to target audiences. Just to give an example, the accent convention, a vital element in stage representations of immigrants, has become a common American theatrical tradition to the point that a so-called dialect coach is responsible for training actors in using a specific stage accent. Jerry Blunt's *Stage Dialects* is one among numerous publications intended as a source of study on foreign dialects and addressed to theatre practitioners. The term commonly used in American theatre to refer to what I have defined accent is 'dialect'. This is how Blunt defines it:

> A dialect is a distinctive form of pronunciation, language structure, and vocabulary which is identified with a geographical area or a social class. ... Further, a dialect is created whenever anyone speaks in a language not his own. Although such speech is often referred to as a foreign accent, it is one more form of dialectal expression. (Blunt, 1967: 1)

Stage Dialect provides the actor with all the following data about each dialect: 'vowel substitutions, dipthongal changes, consonant substitutions, special pronunciations and pitch patterns', together with syntactical and grammatical traits. Blunt also specifies that a stage dialect is 'a normal dialect altered as needed to fit the requirements of theatrical clarity and dramatic interpretation' and characterised by 'factual truthfulness through fidelity to its primary sources and artistic truthfulness through fidelity to a dramatic interpretation'. The most fascinating aspect of the definition of a stage dialect is its exotic nature. Blunt claims that a dialect is distinctive, is different, and therefore this is what makes it attractive and why it is adopted in theatre. The stronger the dialect the more attractive it becomes. Blunt argues that Italian is the most 'distinctive' of all the dialects heard in the United States. Furthermore, in his view, a dialect provides a play with 'dramatic enrichment'.[9]

---

[9] Blunt recognises that as a consequence of the historical process through which immigrants arrived to the United States and struggled to learn English, 'the concept of most Americans as to what makes authentic dialect is based upon the speech of the uneducated immigrant rather than that of the educated foreigner.' (1967: 116) But he also believes that for this reason the best dialects can only be found in the United States and he even regrets that modern education will put an end to the live sources of the accent convention.

Given the political nature of Fo and Rame's theatre, the implications of theatrical traditions become even more evident and acquire further significance. All factors analysed in this chapter, the use of literal translations of the dramatic text and their subsequent adaption, target theatrical traditions, such acting styles and the accent convention, together with cultural images, are part of common practices and approaches which tend to legitimise the appropriation of Fo and Rame's plays in English-speaking countries, as will emerge from the present study.

Chapter 2

Staging Political Theatre

Theatre that sets out to
Please our taste
Often turns out to be a waste of space.
To do its job the theatre has
to risk displeasure
It must provoke, instruct
And entertain in equal
Measure
(Samuel Johnson)

As previously argued, the meaning and significance of political theatre has become highly problematic and open to question. The fuzziness of the category of political theatre will be specifically addressed in this chapter to demonstrate how it can be a pretext to justify the appropriation of foreign texts. More precisely, when looking at translation of political plays, we need to take into account two different perspectives at the same time: the meaning and role of political theatre in the source culture on the one hand and the significance of political theatre in the target theatrical and cultural system. This is why the first part of this chapter focuses on the peculiarities of Fo and Rame's revolutionary theatre within the Italian political context as well as analysing those political plays unknown in English-speaking countries to investigate the reasons for such neglect. The second part of the chapter looks at common practices of appropriation of foreign political theatre in English which equally affect Fo and Rame and Bertolt Brecht's plays.

Since Erwin Piscator (1980) first introduced this definition, political theatre has taken different forms. These include the left-wing agitprop theatre of the 1930s, didactic and revolutionary in its aims, the alternative theatre of the 1960s, which continued the legacy of agitprop to various extents, together with current practices of political theatre, such as community theatre, gay theatre, black theatre, which specifically address issues of gender, race and cultural discrimination. If on the one hand, political theatre is this umbrella definition covering a wide range of theatre practices, the definition itself has been questioned in a number of ways. Augusto Boal argues that all theatre is by definition political given that all human activities, including theatre, are political. Dario Fo similarly claims: 'Lo vado ripetendo da un pezzo: il "teatro politico" non è che un'invenzione di comodo o uno slogan facile. Si può parlare d'amore e fare della politica, dipende da che taglio dai, che valori metti in risalto nel rapporto fra un uomo e una donna' (Fo, 1990).[1] Post-structuralist and post-modern theories similarly argue that all theatre, more precisely all art and culture, are political. Broadly speaking, different views of the notion of political theatre can be reduced to two main ways of conceiving political theatre. In the first instance, we have a 'traditional' notion that identifies as political those plays with a political content, dealing with political and social issues, such as government corruption and racial discrimination. In the second case, the political nature of theatre is defined according to its ability to critique and challenge the status quo and, in Janelle Reinelt's words, to encourage spectators to 'grasp their positioning as individual and collective subjects and regain a capacity to act and struggle' (Reinelt, 1998: 288).

Such distinction corresponds to the difference between politics of content on the one hand and politics of form and function on the other, as identified by Graham Holderness (1992). In his view, the politics of content of a play, the fact that it deals with a political issue, is not effective if its form and function reinforce the dominant ideology. On the contrary a theatre which is provocative in its form and function, for example, by challenging the traditional relation between audience and performance, is politically more progressive. Similarly, Baz Kershaw argues that politically effective theatre is a theatre which may have 'immediate effects on the general historical evolution of wider social and political realities' (Kershaw, 1992).

Hal Foster (1985) makes a distinction between transgressive and resistant politics, a distinction also adopted by Philip Auslander in his analysis of postmodern American performance (1992). Transgressive politics were pursued by modernist avant-garde dramatists of the early twentieth century, such as Piscator and Brecht, who believed that it was possible to transgress the limits of the social realities surrounding them. But postmodernism has shown that such transgression is impossible since no cultural action can go beyond the context in which it is produced, therefore the politics of postmodern performance can only be resistant within the dominant. Postmodernist political art must use the same forms of representation as any other cultural expression while at the same time questioning such means of representation and the ideology behind them. The present analysis reflects the transition from the transgressive politics of 1930s left-wing agitprop theatre and 1960s alternative theatre, examined in this and the next chapter, to the resistant approach of some postmodern productions looked at in the final chapter.

Having said that, despite the fuzziness and limits of the notion of political theatre, it continues to be used by theatre directors, actors, playwrights, and in critical and public response to theatre events (reviews, theatre programmes, advertising material). Precisely because there is no such a thing as a single, comprehensive definition of political theatre, it is always necessary to consider who is using the definition, when and for what purpose. When it comes to the

---

[1] 'I have been saying this for a long time: "political theatre" is nothing more than a handy invention, an easy slogan. You can make politics while talking about love, it depends on your perspective, on the values that you want to emphasise in the relationship between a man and a woman.'

interpretation and reproduction of political plays across cultures, the significance of political theatre depends even more on the cultural and historical perspectives being considered.

Critics and scholars have often emphasised the uniqueness of Fo and Rame's theatre. Chiara Valentini writing for *Panorama* in 1973 argued that their theatre is unique in that it is capable of causing unpredictable reactions, from enthusiasm to political hatred that go beyond the realm of the artistic. What is relevant for the purposes of the present analysis is precisely the impact that Fo and Rame's theatre, marked by a complex combination of left-wing political activism with a rich theatrical and cultural heritage, has had, and continues to have even now, in Italy. For this reason it will be useful at this point to focus on the history of Fo and Rame's theatre to better understand, among other things, its role within the Italian political context.

As has often been noted, Rame comes from a family, whose theatrical history goes back to the eighteenth century, while Fo first graduated in architecture and later got involved in theatre. He started by performing his comic monologues, *Poer Nano*, first for the radio and then for the stage. In 1953 Fo formed a review company with Franco Parenti and Giustino Durano, 'I Dritti', and this was the time when Fo was trained by the French mime Jacques Lecoq, who had a strong influence on him. After getting married in 1954, Fo and Rame founded a company called 'Fo-Rame'. From the late 1950s to the late 1960s they performed in mainstream theatres. Together with their critics, they identify those years as the 'bourgeois period' to distinguish it from the period following the student movements of 1968 when Fo and Rame devoted their work to the working class. In those years they created a theatre collective called 'Nuova Scena' to support the cause of the 1969 revolution. Rather than playing in bourgeois venues, they started to perform in alternative spaces managed by ARCI, the Communist Party's cultural clubs.

Italy in 1969 was dominated by a mass movement of workers who fought for and, in most cases, obtained better wages and better working conditions on an unprecedented scale. Striking was the most common form of protest. Factory workers, in particular, besides going on strike, tended to occupy their factory to make their protest more effective. This is the time when Fo and Rame started to perform to thousands of workers, housewives, unemployed people in improvised venues, such as stadiums, factories, public squares, and actively shared with them their political struggles on stage. 'Nuova Scena', which defined itself as 'un collettivo di militanti ... al servizio della lotta di classe e delle battaglie socialiste' (1970: 9)[2] was determined to create a new revolutionary theatre with precise aims and objectives, such as 'necessità di verificare le proposte ogni sera con tutto il pubblico attraverso un libero dibattito; modifica degli spettacoli attraverso il rapporto dialettico reale instaurato con il pubblico che da fruitore passivo dello spettacolo tende a trasformarsi in compartecipe di scelte politiche e di ipotesi

---

[2] 'A collective of militants ... at the service of the class struggle and of the socialist struggles.'

politiche.' (1970: 9)[3] Their shows were therefore constantly affected and shaped by the interaction with the audience. The heated political debates following their performances represented a 'third act', which became an integral part of those performances. These debates often went on until late at night and represented a unique opportunity for workers to express their views and make their cause known. As a political choice, 'Nuova Scena' decided to perform mainly in small centres and villages in the suburbs rather than in the main Italian cities. A perfect example of Fo and Rame's political commitment is the support they gave to a group of workers who risked losing their jobs because the owner of the factory was going to shut it down. The workers contacted Fo and Rame asking for help. One of them, who intended to start his own business, owned 10,000 glasses and Rame suggested that 'Nuova Scena' could help by trying to sell them after their performances. The following day the glasses were literally taken to the performance venue and one of the factory workers announced their problems to an audience of around 10,000 people. Before the end of the show all the glasses had been sold.

Most important of all, 'Nuova Scena' aimed at creating an alternative theatre circuit with other theatre groups, both amateur and professional, addressed to a large audience, particularly people who had never been to the theatre before, who would have an active role in the staging of political plays. Little by little Fo and Rame's performances and debates with the audience started to affect their relationship with the Communist Party for a number of reasons. Above all, Fo and Rame's criticisms of the PCI, included in plays such as *The Worker Knows 300 Words, the Boss Knows 1000 – That's Why He Is the Boss* (*L'operaio conosce 300 parole, il padrone 1000: per questo lui è il padrone*) and *Tie Me Up but I'll Still Smash Everything* (*Legami pure che tanto spacco tutto lo stesso*), revealed a growing gap between Fo and Rame's views and the Party's positions at a time when the contrast between the latter and left-wing extremist groups also became quite evident. Fo and Rame's performances were strongly attacked in the Party's newspaper *l'Unità* and the PCI tried to hamper their shows in many ways. Furthermore, their theatre started to be opposed by the Italian government. 'Nuova Scena was set up as a private association from the very beginning to avoid the interference of the 'public powers', of censorship and above all to allow debates to take place without any form of constraint. But despite the private nature of the association, the presence of the police under one pretext or another became more and more common. As 'Nuova Scena' argued: 'La macchina repressiva del sistema è già in atto: si incomincia a contestare il carattere privato delle manifestazioni e a usare l'arma della intimidazione nei confronti dei proprietari o gestori dei locali con la minaccia del ritiro della licenza di pubblico esercizio' (1970: 14).[4]

---

[3] 'The need to verify proposals every night with the audience through a free debate; updating of the shows through a true dialectic relationship with the spectators who, instead of being passive customers, become active participants in the making of political choices and political hypothesis.'
[4] 'The system's repressive machine is at work: they have started to question the private nature of activities and to use the weapon of intimidation against owners and managers of venues threatening to withdraw their licence.'

In 1970 Fo and Rame formed a new cooperative, 'La Comune', named after the French working class 'Commune'. They were now based in an old *capannone,* a workshop, in Via Colletta, in Milan. This is when the best known and most performed plays were written and put on stage, such as *Mistero Buffo, Accidental Death of an Anarchist* and *Can't Pay? Won't Pay!. Accidental Death of an Anarchist,* in particular, dealt with the 1969 terrorist attack in Piazza Fontana, in Milan, which killed sixteeen people and wounded over eighty. This was one of several terrorist attacks of which left-wing extremist and anarchist groups were accused, but later proved to be committed by right-wing factions. The late sixties and early seventies represent a complex period of Italian history marked not only by social discontent but also by the so-called *strategy of tension.* As it was made clear in *Accidental Death of an Anarchist,* most of the 173 bomb attacks of those years had been organised by fascist groups and by the Right to discredit the Left. 'La Comune' aimed precisely at questioning and reacting against such political strategy by providing 'counterinformation' through its theatre. Fo and Rame had been asked to write a play about the Milan bomb attack as an opportunity to analyse and discuss the political implications of such events and to compensate for a lack of information in the Italian press.

Those were the years, as Farrell and Scuderi rightly argue (2000), when Fo, influenced by Antonio Gramsci's views on popular culture, created a popular theatre which adopted a Marxist philosophy, was rooted in the tradition of medieval *giullari* and aimed at being revolutionary. Fo describes himself as a modern *giullare, giullare* being the Italian word for medieval street performers who through their satirical performances commented on the experience of ordinary people and attacked the authorities. Fo also emphasises the influence of the *fabulatori,* storytellers from the Lake Maggiore region where he grew up. For a long time he was exposed to the stories recounted by local fishermen and artisans who combined true events with fantastical tales. Like the *fabulatori,* Fo concentrates on the story that he is telling his audience. His theatre focuses on the content, on the story rather than the characters inhabiting the story. Fo defines his theatre as 'a theatre of situation', the situation being the basic structure of a narrative organised in such a way as to ensure the participation of the audience (Fo, 1997). As Rame puts it, when Fo writes:

> he needs to think out and build a stage, or preferably, a sequence of scenic spaces and planes on which the dramatic action can take place. It is also a question of theatrical construction rather than simple writing because his theatre is not based on characters, but on situations. The characters become masks, i.e. emblematic pretexts at the service of a situation. (1994b: xxviii-xxix)

Fo and Rame's satire, which has the ability to ridicule those in power while at the same time being incredibly hilarious, has cost them the opposition of the Italian government and the Church, numerous cases of censorship and lawsuits, imprisonment, hatred from various political factions, intellectuals and critics, even kidnapping and rape by a group of fascists in the case of Rame. Their commitment to political activism has been misinterpreted as being supportive of terrorist groups, such as the Red Brigades, both in Italy and abroad. As will be shown in chapter four, on three occasions Fo and Rame were denied a visa to enter the United States because of their involvement with an organization called 'Soccorso Rosso', created by Rame, to help families of political prisoners. Far from supporting terrorist acts, Fo and Rame on the contrary have been subject to violence and censorship because they have fought and continue to fight against corrupt governments and repressive laws.

For all the above reasons it is paramount to understand the uniqueness of Fo and Rame's political theatre, as being strictly related to specific historical circumstances in Italy, such as the years of terrorism, as well as being the product of a classical theatrical tradition dating back to Aristophanes. Specific references to Italian political events and political figures inevitably represent considerable obstacles to the translation of their plays into different cultural contexts, despite the fact that numerous issues, such as police violence, have global resonance rather than being limited to Italy. Furthermore, as shown in the previous chapter, Fo and Rame's satire, combining a number of theatrical styles and traditions, including *commedia dell'arte*, circus techniques and Bertolt Brecht's Epic Theatre, constitutes yet another obstacle to the staging of their work in other countries with different theatrical traditions and actor training.

Having said that, they have performed for thousands of Italian and foreign spectators and their theatre has been translated and staged throughout the world. This book shows exactly how such success has been achieved despite the above-mentioned difficulties. More precisely, their success in English-speaking countries is based on a limited and careful selection of plays, such as *Accidental Death of an Anarchist* and *Can't Pay? Won't Pay!* Whereas the latter are Fo and Rame's best known plays, other political plays written around the same period, between the late 1960s and early 1970s, such as *The Worker Knows 300 Words, The Boss 1000 – That's Why He's the Boss, United We Stand! All Together Now! (Tutti uniti! Tutti insieme! Ma scusa, quello non è il padrone?), The Boss's Funeral (Il funerale del padrone)* are little known or have never been staged in English. It might be helpful to look at these plays to understand the difficulties of translating and staging them for English-speaking audiences.

The Worker Knows 300 Words, The Boss 1000 – That's Why He's the Boss is set in the library of a working men's club, where a group of workers are tidying up and clearing out books to make way for pool tables. Going through the books the workers come across and discuss the politics of revolutionary figures, such as Gramsci and the Soviet poet and playwright Mayakovsky, together with the Stalinist trials of the Czech activist Slansky. In other words, this becomes an opportunity for the workers to discover their own history and culture. Through the play Fo attacks a social context whereby workers are denied access to their own culture and are therefore prevented from having an active role within their party and society at large. While David Hirst defines the play as 'one of the most original, fascinating and underestimated of Fo's works' (Hirst, 1989: 174), Tony Mitchell argues that the weakness of the play lies in its 'highly doctrinaire Marxist line' (Mitchell, 1999: 95). This goes with the fact that the play deals more with a theoretical matter than a specific political issue, that is to say the role of culture, and theatre, as the basis of working class political awareness. Moreover, as emphasised by Tom Behan[5] among other scholars, *The Worker Knows 300 Words* is a serious play with hardly any comedy in it. It even includes a monologue about the story of Michele Lu Lanzone, a Sicilian union leader who fought against the Mafia. The story is narrated by the mother and introduced by the music of a guitar. As explained in the published text, the actress, who is required to play all the roles, including that of Michele, should perform 'in the epic style', due to the highly emotional nature of the story.

The Worker Knows 300 Words was staged at the Latchmere Theatre from 21 March to 7 April 1985, in a translation by David Hirst with 'additional material' by the Yorick Theatre Company, directed by Michael Batz. In her review Sheila Fox argued that, despite having been written shortly before *Accidental Death*, the play 'shows the flip-side of Dario Fo – what remains when the brilliant, anarchic wit and slap-stick belligerance are left tossing on the high seas without any coherent dramatic structure to anchor them' (Fox, 1985). Similarly, Ann McFerran criticised the 'over-schematic structure, which at times feels like a political lecture with slides' and added: 'Unfortunately this is a long winded piece where much of the dialogue consists of uninspired sloganisings and it is visually extremely dull; the production is unweildly and lacks depth and pace' (McFerran, 1985). Such a negative critical response was not only due to the didactic structure of the play, but was also reinforced by the material added by the Yorick Company. Desmond Christy in the *Guardian* lamented the addition of

> a cabaret act of a grotesque Mrs. Thatcher dancing with Ronald Reagan (he presents her with a present of a cruise missile) and the Pope dancing the life out of Solidarity. This is what now passes for satire on television. It's a pity to see a fringe theatre borrowing from the box. (…) At the moment this is very English agitprop. (Christy, 1985)

Rather than making the play more suitable to British audiences, the scenes added by the Yorick Company were perceived as being external to the performance and therefore affected the reception of the play, as shown by the above mentioned review.

Behan has recently adapted a number of plays, including *The Worker Knows 300 Words*. Behan's approach is to relocate Fo plays to the UK, as in the case of *The Worker Knows 300 Words*, set within the context of a trade union of mineworkers. He has similarly transposed the monologue of Michele Lu Lanzone to the British mineworkers' strike and in his translation it is the mother of a mineworker killed during a demonstration who narrates the story. Behan has also translated and adapted *The Boss's Funeral*, a one-act play originally staged together as part of *Legami Pure*, which included another one-act play *The Loom* (*Il Telaio*). In *The Boss's Funeral* a group of workers occupy a factory and having been evicted by the police, decide to stage a carnivalesque play about the funeral of their boss to draw attention to their cause. The play is a satire of the industrial pollution and the working conditions to which workers were subject in Italian

---

[5] Telephone interview with Tom Behan, April 2004.

factories. It ends with a scene, where a worker is supposed to be executed in order to fulfil the daily quota of industrial accidents, which is then replaced by that of a butcher killing a goat. The debate among the actors about the use of such a theatrical device develops into a debate with the audience about the killing of the goat, which concludes the performance. Although the French theatre critic Bernard Dort praised the philosophical connotations of the play (Dort, 1997), its simple structure and agitprop nature cannot be denied. As Mario Mignone argues, both *The Boss's Funeral* and *The Loom* testify to the emphasis that at the time Fo put on the 'didactic and polemical value' of its theatre, 'over and above its purely aesthetic qualities' (Mignone, 1981: 56). There was only one British production of *The Boss's Funeral* at Essex University Theatre on 27 March 1987, in a translation by David Hirst, directed by Chris Adamson, but there was no press coverage. Behan's adaptation has not been staged yet.

United *We Stand! All Together Now!*, with the subtitle *Workers' Struggles 1911-1922*, tells the story of the transformation of Antonia, who becomes a revolutionary activist after her husband, Norberto, a militant of the Italian Socialist Party, is killed by fascists. The play deals with the Italian workers' movement, the role of the Socialist Party and the Communist Party which was created in those years. The character of Antonia is a *commedia dell'arte* character, called *étourdie*, a vamp who makes an intelligent use of her role after acquiring a political consciousness. In an article appeared in *Sipario*, Fo explained that the play was his response to the workers' limited knowledge of the years of Fascism and their need, expressed in meetings and discussions with Fo and Rame, to fully understand the significance of that period of Italian history, which was connected with the appearance of the workers' movement (Fo, 1971). In Mitchell's view, this is 'one of Fo's more didactic plays' given its use of placards, songs and political discussions (Mitchell, 1999: 115). Similarly, Lanfranco Binni argues that *United We Stand! All Together Now!* is different from the other plays of the same period, like *Accidental Death of an Anarchist*, because of its didactic structure, its slow pace which give the impression that its story, rather than being represented on stage, is simply narrated (Binni, 1975).

In 1972 Fo wrote and staged a continuation of *Accidental Death of an Anarchist*, entitled *Knock Knock! Who's There? Police! (Pum, pum! Chi è? La polizia!) Knock Knock!* dealt with the police corruption involved in the investigation about the Piazza Fontana bombing, but included the events which followed the staging of *Accidental Death of an Anarchist*. Like the previous play, *Knock Knock!* documented legal cases as they were taking place and for this reason Fo and Rame continued to be put under pressure by the police and the political establishment. Nevertheless, there is a considerable difference between the two plays, since *Knock Knock!* is a sort of documentary play, which by definition focuses on providing information to the audience, and lacks the farcical structure of the previous play. It is set at the Ministry of Internal Affairs and the protagonists of the staged events are identified through their real names. This is probably the reason why while *Accidental Death of an Anarchist* is one of Fo and Rame's best known and most successful plays, *Knock Knock!* was never translated nor staged in English. As will be shown in chapter four, it is precisely the theatrical quality of

Accidental Death of an Anarchist that turned it into a West End hit, whereas the prevailing documentary nature of its sequel constituted an unsurmountable obstacle to its transposition into a foreign context.

Few years later, in 1976, Fo and Rame staged *Mum's Marijuana is the Best*. It is the story of a grandfather, played by Fo, and a mother, played by Rame, from a working class family, who pretend to be drug addicts and dealers after finding out that their son/grandson Luigi smokes marijuana, in order to teach him a lesson. The play is an attack against the Italian government for failing to deal with the drug problem on a social and cultural as well as medical level. As Ugo Volli argued, 'Importante, e radicalmente nuovo nell'ambito della sinistra extraparlamentare, è l'accento posto sul carattere culturale della questione della droga ... anche come mediazione tra problema personale e prospettiva politica' (Volli, 1976).[6] In other words, the drug problem is addressed from a class perspective and set within the local political context, marked by a crisis of the revolutionary left. This means that despite the general relevance of its theme, the play was strictly linked to the Italian political environment of the time. Mitchell's translation, commissioned by the same company which staged *Accidental Death*, Belt and Braces, was never put on stage. In Mitchell's view, this was due to the fact that the company was busy with the transfer of *Accidental Death* to the West End, as well as to 'the difficulty of making the play relevant to English audiences' (Mitchell, 1999: 145). In Volli's words, the play was a 'farsa didascalica ... finalizzata ad una chiave strettamente politico-didattica', and 'lo spettacolo deve sopportare frequenti pause di azione, in cui i personaggi parlano, spiegano, polemizzano, si stanno ad ascoltare.' (Volli, 1976)[7] This means that both the content of the play, given that its analysis of the drug problem could not be separated from its political references, and its didactic structure makes its staging on a foreign stage problematic.

Having said that, there was a rehearsed reading of Behan's adaptation of *Mum's Marijuana is the Best* at the Playroom on 27 April 2000 as part of the Fo–Rame conference in Cambridge organised by Ed Emery. The entrance was free but a mimum donation of £3 was suggested since it was a benefit performance for the 'Cambridge Two/Wintercomfort Defence Campaign', to support the workers of a hostel for the homeless sentenced to four and five years' imprisonment (135 pounds were raised). Besides adapting the play, Behan also performed in the Cambridge reading. Needless to say, the reading was seen by an elite audience, since most were scholars and admirers of Fo and Rame's work. A reduced-length production of the same adaptation was staged for three nights in July 2000 at the Socialist Workers Party annual conference on Marxism in London by the Stuffed Hamster Theatre Company. The performance lasted just 45 minutes since, as specified in the programme some scenes were cut, and the actors had limited time

---

[6] 'The accent put on the cultural nature of the drugs issue is important and completely new in the context of the extra-parliamentary left-wing ... , also because it represents a middle course between a personal problem and a political perspective.'

[7] 'A didactic farce ... aimed at a strictly political-didactic perspective, whereby the show is subject to frequent pauses of action, during which the characters talk, explain, argue, listen to each other.'

to rehearse. Finally, there was a full-length production by final year drama students of the University of Kent, at the Gulbenkian Theatre, Canterbury, on 19 March 2003. According to Behan, this staging succeeded in being funny, as testified by the audience's reaction.[8]

Behan wrote some interesting comments about his adaptation and involvement with the stagings of the play in *The Times Higher Educational Supplement*. He has set the play in Blair's Britain, more precisely in a working class estate in Hackney and has inserted references to Mandelson, Alastair Campbell and to local issues, such as London transport. He has also adapted it to the style of English farce, as in one scene where he has placed 'Alastair Campbell up a priest's arse, with a bright white light shining out' (Behan, 2000b). In his view, in the London reduced-length production there was 'symmetry in terms of the venue and the audience' (Behan, 2000b). Behan expected some reviews given that the organiser had contacted '120 media outlets' and that, as he emphasises, 'after all, this is the English première of a play by the world's leading radical dramatist. This diary is the first public comment on the event.' Unfortunately there was no press coverage of any of the above-mentioned productions, and given that the London staging ran for three nights and that there was only one student performance at Canterbury, they inevitably reached a rather limited audience.

All of the reading/performances of *Mum's Marijuana* were based on Behan's adaptation and they took place thanks to his interest in Fo and Rame's work. Behan, like Chiara Valentini (1977), admits that the weakness of the play lies in the fact that it does not have a precise and recognisable target, unlike most of Fo's theatre, combined with the fact that its argument, that marijuana is not harmful, is out of date. Furthermore, *Mum's Marijuana*, together with the previously mentioned plays, which deal more or less directly with the Italian workers' movement and the history of the Italian left, share a didactic structure, as emphasised in the Italian critical response. This sets them apart from other Fo and Rame's plays, such as *Accidental Death of an Anarchist*, whose balanced combination of a political content with a coherent dramatic form represents the unique mark of their theatre. The 'secret' behind the success of a number of Fo and Rame's plays lies precisely in such unusual mixing of comedy and politics and the way in which it is transformed when translated into foreign languages.

This explains why, on the contrary, plays such as *United We Stand! All Together Now!*, dealing with political issues through didactic forms, do not appeal to foreign audiences and are therefore not seen on British and American stages. Most important of all, as previously argued, those plays were the specific product of a time of political and social turmoil when there was a strong demand for political education. Their didactic nature resulted from a common need to stimulate discussion, particularly among the working class, and was therefore appreciated by the audience. If we consider that a number of Fo and Rame's spectators had never been to the theatre before seeing their shows and that in a number of cases they went to see the same performance for two consecutive nights to develop the

---

[8] Telephone interview with Tom Behan, April 2004.

discussion further, it becomes clear that the nature of these plays cannot be separated from the political situation in which they were embedded. This means that when they are taken out of their original context and staged at a different time and in a country with a different political atmosphere, they are bound to lose their political function and therefore to be simply reduced to dull and didactic theatre texts.

Having considered the reasons why some of Fo and Rame's political plays are neglected, we should now look at common practices of appropriation to which foreign political plays, not only those by Fo and Rame, are subject in the United Kingdom and the United States. Some of these are: the use of the definition of political theatre as a tool to justify the appropriation of foreign texts according to the dominant values of the receiving society; a tendency to separate the political from the theatrical aspects of foreign plays and to downplay the first in order to emphasise the second; an interpretation of foreign texts based on commonly shared stereotypical notions of the foreign culture they come from.

These become apparent if we look at the following two reviews:

> The history of the reception of Brecht in Britain is an embarrassing one. A series of imbalances, of half-aware ideas about the purposes of Brecht's practical dramaturgy, were made worse by a far more influential misconception about his politics and the significance of his politics for his drama. It is to a large extent through a refusal to accept the fundamentally political bias of Brecht's theatre practice that critics have created the illusory split of Brecht into a good playwright and a bad politician. (Holland, 1978: 24)

> So far, most productions of *Anarchist* have tried to downplay or ignore the politics. Producers, directors and players have aimed for a slapstick hit. Their thinking seems to be that the more the play is de-politicized, the better will be its reception from the public and the critics. (Davis, 1986: 313)

In other words, when translated into English, the politics of function of Bertolt Brecht, Fo and Rame's theatre are reduced to politics of content and this equally applies to the production and reception of their theatre. In the same way as directors and actors focus on the comic aspects of their plays, critics equally downplay their political role. Such an approach is directly linked to the history of political theatre in both the United Kingdom and the United States and it testifies to the influence that target culture notions of theatre have on the reception of foreign plays.

André Lefevere has identified four different strategies adopted by British and American rewriters of Brecht's theatre to make it less challenging and more acceptable. It is interesting to briefly look at such strategies since they similarly apply, to a certain extent, to Fo and Rame's work. According to the first one, Brecht's plays are valued with no concern for his theoretical approach to theatre, such as his theory of alienation; the second strategy has been defined by Lefevere as 'the psychological cop-out', i.e. audiences should concentrate on his plays rather than his ideology; the third denies the novelty and originality of Brecht's statements, and the fourth is based on the assumption that traditional practices of theatre, such as Realism, are perfectly compatible with Brecht's plays. It is fascinating to see how often the second strategy identified by Lefevere, usually combined with the first, is adopted by critics reviewing productions of Brecht's work in English, and how a denial of Brecht's political, and theoretical views, is presented to British and American readers and theatre-goers as the way to 'liberate' Brecht's texts and allow them to be enjoyable plays.

In his review of William Gaskill's production of *Mother Courage and Her Children* in 1965, based on Eric Bentley's translation, Young refuses Brecht's notion of alienation because it 'removes the principal quality on which theatre depends, the ability to involve the audience in the emotions generated by the actors' and concludes: 'Because behind the pedant there was a dramatist screaming to get out, humanity kept breathing in. One day perhaps a producer will come along prepared to jettison all the Brechtian paraphernalia and produce his plays as if they were plays and not textbooks' (1965). Brecht is portrayed as having a split personality, as a pedant that prevents the dramatist from expressing himself. But Young has a solution at hand: a producer who ignores Brecht's ideological position. It goes without saying that this insistence on the split between politics and theatre in the British and American reception of foreign political playwrights raises significant ideological issues and that the priority given to the theatricality over the politics is a sign of the process of manipulation that such plays undergo in the United Kingdom and the United States.

The impact of the fourth strategy can be explained in terms of the relation between foreign plays and the target theatrical system. As previously argued, the theatrical practices and traditions of the receiving culture determine the ways in which foreign plays are put on stage. For example, given that Realism is the dominant aspect of British and American theatrical traditions, in both countries directors tend to adopt a realistic interpretation of Brecht, as well as Fo and Rame's work, despite the 'epic' nature of their theatre. When Howard Davies staged *Man is Man* for the Royal Shakespeare Company in 1975 at the Other Place in Stratford, he made it clear that he looked for realism in the play and that he saw the soldiers as real, everyday characters, rather than cruel and violent expressions of a reactionary state (Eddershaw, 1996). The similarities between the reception of Fo and Brecht's work are striking. In the 1979 production of *Accidental Death of an Anarchist* Gavin Richards turned the aggressive and incompetent policemen of the Italian play into innocuous stock characters with silly names, such as Inspector Pissani. In 1984 *Mother Courage* was staged at the Barbican Theatre, in a translation by Hanif Kureishi, who aimed at turning 'a long, tedious, stodgy anti-war play into something warm and funny' (Kureishi, 1984). In this sense, Kureishi adhered to the previously analysed tendency to emphasise the comedy of foreign plays, which is equally evident in the reception of other playwrights.

What is important to stress here is that the split between the ideological and political aspects of these plays and the fact that their humour is emphasised over and over again by critics and theatre professionals is the result of the British and American theatrical and cultural interpretation of them, rather than one of their inherent qualities. As Susan Bassnett argues, no author is more translatable than another since translatability depends on a variety of cultural factors, as well as marketing issues (Bassnett, 2000: 12). British and American theatrical traditions and constraints, together with Anglo-American preconceptions about German culture, affect Brecht's plays to the point of making them appear as heavy and didactic. Harold Hobson makes this clear:

> The poverty of British productions of Brecht, heavy, sententious, and void of life, was exposed by the Berliner Ensemble when it came to one of Peter Daubeny's World Theatre Seasons, and played *The Resistible Rise of Arturo Ui* with verve, melodramatic vigour, and regard for theatrical effect as well as doctrinal orthodoxy. (1984)

This cannot be separated from the common image of Brecht as a boring German playwright, as emphasised by Robert Hanks: 'It is notable how often people tell you that Brecht should be entertaining. Partly that's a reaction to a long British tradition of regarding anything German as humourless and didactic – honest, they're saying, you'll enjoy this' (Hanks, 1995). So, for example, for the 1995 National Theatre production of *Mother Courage* at the Olivier, based on David Hare's translation, the marketing strategy was clear: producers tried to attract British audiences by promising a very different Brecht from the one presented by previous stagings: funny and even sexy (Spencer, 1995).

Another central issue to bear in mind is that, as will be shown later in relation to the 1979 first British staging of Dario Fo's *Accidental Death of an Anarchist*, the first successful productions of a foreign playwright, staged in mainstream theatres, can acquire a certain authority to the point where they become the 'original' to which subsequent productions are compared. More often than not, critics base their reviews of a given production on their experience of the previous 'authoritative' production without knowing the source text. As Margaret Eddershaw argues, British reviews of Brecht's productions reveal critics' concern for fidelity to the text as well as to preconceptions of what Brechtian practice is (Eddershaw, 1996: 97). For example, the fact that in April 1990 Michael Billington wrote in the *Guardian* that one can enjoy Brecht's dramaturgy without his ideology and that 'Brecht's artistry is bigger than his Marxism' indicates that his perception of Brecht's work had not changed much since the late 1950s (Billington, 1990). This means that the political nature of Brecht's work has been and continues to be undermined and distorted to fit in with the target social and theatrical exigencies.

We have seen that political theatre, precisely because of its complex identity, precisely because of the overuse and abuse of such notion, is even more clearly subject than other forms of theatre to a process of Anglicisation and Americanisation. In other words, political theatre seems to provide a justification for being assimilated into the target system that is commonly accepted by the receiving culture, i.e. the need to turn serious and didactic plays into plays that can entertain domestic audiences. In 1998 Billington argued that among a series of factors against Brecht's theatre in the United Kingdom, such as the cost to stage his plays, the most prominent one is that his plays 'require alert audience and directors ready to have their assumptions challenged' (Billington, 1998). Hence, while the principle that foreign plays should be adapted to satisfy the taste and theatrical habits of target theatre-goers is a general one that seems to govern British and American productions, such principle becomes even more evident when it comes to Fo and Rame's political plays because the undermining of their political efficacy makes their assimilation even more significant and ideologically questionable, as will be shown in the following chapters.

Chapter 3

Fo and Rame on the British Stage

Mitchell (1999) argues that Fo is the most widely performed playwright in the world. In Europe, Fo and Rame's plays have been performed since the 1960s and 1970s, particularly in Denmark, Belgium, France, Spain, Sweden and Germany. The popularity of their work in the United Kingdom, where it was introduced between the end of the 1970s and the beginning of the 1980s, is unusual in that it sets unprecedented records of success. In the summer of 1981 three of their plays were being performed at the same time in London, two of them in the West End: *Accidental Death of an Anarchist*[1] in its third year at the Albery Theatre, *Can't Pay? Won't Pay!* at the Criterion[2] and *One Woman Plays (Tutta casa, letto e chiesa)* at the National Theatre.[3] In the following years two more plays were staged in the West End: *Trumpets and Raspberries (Clacson, trombette e pernacchi)* at the Phoenix Theatre in 1984[4] and *The Pope and the Witch (Il papa e la strega)* in 1992.[5] Such popularity makes the history of Fo and Rame's work in the United Kingdom a fascinating case study.

A brief analysis of British political theatre will allow us to contextualise Fo and Rame's work within the target theatrical system and to address claims about a lack of politically challenging comedies in the UK which, as will be shown, functions as a pretext to emphasise the otherness of Fo and Rame's theatre. The above-mentioned stagings will be examined in this chapter to show how their success was

---

[1] The production opened at Dartington College of Arts, Devon, in February 1979 and after touring in Northern England transferred to the Half Moon, London in October 1979. It was adapted and directed by Gavin Richards, who based his adaptation on the literal translation by Gillian Hanna.

[2] It was adapted by Bill Colvill and Robert Walker, from a translation by Lino Pertile and directed by Robert Walker. The play was first staged at the Half Moon in May 1978 under the title *We Can't Pay? We Won't Pay!* When it transferred to the Criterion Theatre, in the West End, in July 1981 the title changed to *Can't Pay?, Won't Pay!*

[3] The play was translated by Margaret Kunzle, adapted by Olwen Wymark and directed by Michael Bogdanov. The South African actress Yvonne Bryceland performed the monologues.

[4] *Trumpets and Raspberries* was translated and adapted by Roger McAvoy and Anna Maria Giugni. First performed at the Watford palace in October 1985, it moved to the Phoenix Theatre in November 1985.

[5] Andy de la Tour adapted the play from a literal translation by Ed Emery. The production transferred from the West Yorkshire Playhouse, Leeds to the Comedy Theatre in London and it was directed by Jude Kelly.

achieved by transposing Fo and Rame's political and revolutionary theatre into very different plays. It will be argued that these productions adhered, in different degrees, to a process of Anglicisation of Fo and Rame's plays, which consists of a predominantly comic reading of their work at the expense of its political challenge. It is the combination of the nature of Fo's theatre[6] and the impact of the target cultural and theatrical system which determine such a process of appropriation. The social and political immediacy of his plays, most of which were written as a provocative and active response to Italian events, makes Fo's work unusual and difficult to transplant to foreign countries. When his plays are taken out of the political context in which they originated, the focus of attention shifts from their social, political and ideological relevance to their efficacy as theatre texts. Although in a number of cases Fo's British rewriters try to relate the staging of his plays to local issues, as will be shown in this chapter, the political challenge of Fo's theatre tends to be relegated to a secondary position and to function as an external commentary. The comedy, the entertaining quality of Fo's plays are given priority by British adapters and directors to ensure their assimilation into the receiving society.

The political immediacy of Fo's plays appears to be one of the main obstacles in staging them in the United Kingdom and, for that matter, in any foreign country. As Mitchell (1999) argues, knowledge of Italian events, such as the Piazza Fontana bombings in 1969, the defenestration of the anarchist Giuseppe Pinelli, the imprisonment of Pietro Valpreda, the 'strategy of tension' dominating the Italian political scene of those years, are necessary to understand the significance of *Accidental Death of an Anarchist*. Transferring the specific political references on which Fo's plays are based to foreign contexts, trying to maintain the same immediacy and social relevance of the source texts, constitute the major difficulty that rewriters of Fo's work have to face.

One other element which complicates the process of translation of their plays into foreign languages is that they do not have the permanent value of words fixed on a page, as explained in chapter one. The text of *Accidental Death of an Anarchist*, among others, evolved in parallel with the development of a libel case brought by Luigi Calabresi against the newspaper *Lotta Continua* concerning the death of Pinelli.[7] Fo (1974) has defined his work as 'teatro da bruciare', a

---

[6] Whenever I talk of 'Fo's theatre' or 'Fo's plays' for brevity, it always stands for Fo and Rame's plays. Their theatre is the result of Rame's creative input as much as Fo's and their career and work cannot be separated since they have worked together and influenced each other all their lives.

[7] There are two published editions of the play: 'Morte accidentale di un anarchico', in Collettivo Teatrale La Comune (1973) *Compagni senza censura*, vol. 2. Milan: Mazzotta Editore, pp. 14-182 and Dario Fo (1974) *Morte accidentale di un anarchico*. Turin: Einaudi. According to the prologue of the 1973 edition, the play makes use of an old theatrical device and transfers an event occurred in New York in 1921, i.e. the defenestration of the Italian immigrant Andrea Salsedo, to an Italian city, Milan. This

throwaway theatre, that should stimulate debates and political actions. Thus, although Fo and Rame's work has been published in a 13-volume edition by Einaudi and in one single volume in 2000, translators rarely find themselves dealing with texts that have a stable form; instead they have to confront living organisms always subject to change. This means that in Fo and Rame's theatre the dramatic text mirrors the ephemeral nature of the *mise en scène* in that it evolves and adapts itself to new contexts of performance, even before it is transposed into foreign cultures. But despite these difficulties, the first British professional production of *Accidental Death of an Anarchist* by the socialist theatre group Belt and Braces Roadshow Company, in 1979, directed and adapted by Gavin Richards, was very successful.

Accidental Death of an Anarchist, defined by Fo as 'a grotesque farce about a tragic farce', is based on a real case of Italian police and government corruption related to the years of terrorism. The anarchist Pinelli was wrongly accused of placing a bomb at the Banca Nazionale in Piazza Fontana and, according to the police, died after accidentally falling out of a window at the police headquarters in 1969. The play is lead by the 'Matto', played by Fo, who, after being arrested by the police, does a series of impersonations, including disguising himself as the judge supposed to conduct the investigation on the Pinelli case, reveal the inconsistencies of the police version of Pinelli's death and make them admit to their responsibilities. *Accidental Death* has been performed to thousands of people in Italy, as well as throughout the world.

At the time when the play was first staged in the United Kingdom, farce was becoming more and more popular, not simply as comedy, but as a politically challenging form of theatre. As Jennifer Lorch puts it, 'Gavin Richards's production of *Accidental Death* was timely' (Lorch, 2000: 152). This is one of the reasons for the success of Richards's production and this would explain why *Accidental Death of an Anarchist* had a considerable impact on British theatre. According to Michael Hastings, *Accidental Death of an Anarchist* was one among a number of plays, such as Orton's *What the Butler Saw* and Caryl Churchill's *Cloud Nine*, which resulted from and testified to 'a shared intention among playwrights to treat antic comedy as a weapon' (Hastings, 1979). Although both Hastings and Lorch's points are well taken, this interest in farce among British playwrights explains only partially the huge popularity of *Accidental Death of an Anarchist*, which later transferred to the West End.

It is interesting to note that other British critics often seem to argue the opposite of what Lorch and Hastings claim: their assumption is that Fo's work was filling in a gap in British theatre. In Michael Coveney's opinion, before the Half Moon production of *We Can't Pay? We Won't Pay!* 'left-wing farce was an unknown commodity in London' (1981). Similarly Ros Asquith argued that 'the crafty art of

prologue was cut in 1974. The endings of the two editions are also different, as we will see. These are the main differences between the two texts. Since the passages to which I refer are the same in both editions I refer only to the 1974 Einaudi text.

blending radical politics and high comedy is unthinkable in Britain' (1984) and for this reason praised the introduction of Fo's work in the United Kingdom, defining him as 'a man who happily combines the Marxism of both Harpo and Karl, while remaining mercifully independent of the Kremlin line'. John Connor claimed that political farce cannot be produced in Britain and can only be imported from abroad since it would be unthinkable to see 'a comedy based on the Brighton bombing being staged anywhere in the country, let alone in the West End' (Connor, 1984).

In order to understand and question the basis of the above claims that political farce did not exist in the UK we need to look at the history of British political theatre. In the late 1960s and early 1970s there was a proliferation of alternative theatre companies, which were a product of the counter-culture movement and of the social and political events of 1968.[8] The number of alternative theatre companies grew enormously between 1970 and 1976 and by the second half of the 1980s there were more than 300. These groups produced a theatre of social engagement, which identified itself by its opposition to conventional theatre and was defined as 'experimental', 'underground' and 'fringe'. As Baz Kershaw puts it, the British alternative theatre movement was characterised by a carnivalesque resistance to the status quo (Kershaw, 1992: 73). In particular, a number of groups aimed at providing theatre specifically addressing working class issues, combining agitprop style with popular theatre forms. They performed in small theatre venues, hundreds of which opened in the seventies, including pubs and community centres, and established a direct relation with their audience. While a detailed analysis of British political theatre is beyond the scope of this book, I would like to focus briefly on a number of political theatre groups, some of which played an important role in introducing Fo's, and Brecht's work, to the United Kingdom.

One of the most important theatre companies in the history of British political theatre was CAST (Cartoon Archetypal Slogan Theatre). As Catherine Itzin argues (1980), it was the first socialist group of the sixties and one that set precedents for future political theatre groups. CAST used satire as a political weapon against the establishment in the style of agitprop theatre. CAST's aim was to make political theatre available for widespread consumption and drew on traditions like that of music-hall, as well as television and cinema. CAST's agenda and acting style made their theatre similar to that of Fo since they also tried to educate and stimulate their audience while entertaining them. Ronald Muldoon, founder of the group, played Muggins, a working class clown. Muggins was a comic character with a life of his own and Muldoon was a political ironist who would distance himself from his character to criticise British society, including the working class, an element which is also reminiscent of Fo.

Another important group was the 7:84 Theatre Company, founded by John McGrath in 1971. The company's aim was to create a revolutionary theatre, opposed to bourgeois theatre, 'a theatre of and for the working class in a socialist

---

[8] For a detailed history of political alternative theatre see: John Bull (1984); Catherine Itzin (1980); Sandy Craig (1980); Andrew Davies (1987); Clive Barker (1992).

way', in McGrath's words (1981: 110). The name in fact reflects McGrath's Marxist agenda since it underlines that seven percent of the population owns 84 percent of the wealth. Among other plays, in 1972 7:84 staged *The Ballygombeen Bequest* by John Arden and Margaretta D'Arcy on the issue of land expropriation in Northern Ireland, which was censored and stopped because of a legal action. In 1973 Gavin Richards, a member of 7:84 who had directed *The Ballygombeen Bequest*, created a new company, Belt and Braces, while McGrath started up a Scottish company, 7:84 Scotland, promoting a Marxist analysis of Scottish history. Plays such as *The Cheviot, The Stag and the Black, Black Oil* encouraged resistance to the exploitation which had characterised Scotland's existence for centuries. In this play McGrath made use of a popular theatre form from the Highlands, the *ceilidh* and included songs in Gaelic and English which, in McGrath's opinion, 'went to the root of suppressed popular feeling' (McGrath, 1981: 122).

Belt and Braces aimed at entertaining their audience through popular forms of theatre while supporting the view of the working class and of oppressed members of society. According to Itzin, by 1979 Belt and Braces was one of the most important socialist theatre companies which distinguished itself for dealing with political and economic issues, and they staged both Brecht's and Fo's work (Itzin, 1980: 206). More precisely, Belt and Braces produced *Mother Courage*, in a translation by the playwright Steve Gooch, at the Half Moon in 1973. Robert Walker also directed a production of *The Resistible Rise of Arturo Ui*, adapted by George Tabori, at the Half Moon in 1978, a production of Fo's *We Can't Pay? We Won't Pay!*, adapted by Bill Colvill and Robert Walker, and a staging of *Accidental Death of an Anarchist*, adapted by Gavin Richards, the following year. Another company which staged Fo and Rame's work was the Monstrous Regiment Group. This was founded in 1975 by socialist feminist actresses. The company addressed the condition of women in society by experimenting with different forms of entertainment, such as music as well as cabaret. One of the founders was Gillian Hanna, who made the literal translation of *Accidental Death* on which Richards' adaptation was based, translated *Elizabeth* (*Elisabetta, una donna per caso*)[9] and *Tutta casa, letto e chiesa*, as *The Fourth Wall*, staged by the Monstrous Regiment at the Drill Hall, London in 1983.[10]

The work of the above mentioned groups testifies to the importance of political theatre in the United Kingdom and indicates that, contrary to what some may claim, a politically and socially challenging theatre based on popular culture in the vein of Fo's style was not unknown in the receiving culture. This is also Mitchell's view who, while recognising the difficulties in translating Fo's plays, believes that the main problem is not 'the lack of a comparable tradition of working-class and

---

[9] The production, in which Hanna played the lead role, was staged at the Half Moon Theatre in November 1986 and directed by Michael Batz and Chris Bond.

[10] *The Fourth Wall* included the following four monologues: *I'm Ulrike I'm Screaming*, *Alice in Wonderless Land*, *It Happened Tomorrow* and *The Whore in the Madhouse*.

popular culture in the British theatre' (Mitchell, 1999: 243). Thus, it can be argued that there was a British political theatre tradition in which Fo's work could have fitted, but it is important to stress here that such theatre was very parochial, it focused on very local issues, as previously shown. Needless to say, there are other differences, particularly evident in terms of theatrical traditions and acting style, that need to be taken into account. John McGrath has emphasised the contrast between Fo's style and British theatrical traditions in terms of their heritage:

> I was very struck by the fact that the root of Fo's comedy is peasant, and essentially all the stuff about the body and eating and gluttony, and the wonderful outrage he gets, is a peasant thing. I was also very struck by the fact that our comedy, and our kind of radical entertainment, is industrial and goes back through variety and vaudeville to industrial roots. (McGrath, 1985: 394)

As previously argued, another main difference affecting English-language productions of Fo and Rame's plays is that one of the foundations of their theatre is its epic nature. As Rame emphasised in an interview with Tony Mitchell (1999: 272), the 1981 National Theatre production of *One Woman Plays* was based on an acting style very different from hers and Fo's: 'We always try to eliminate the superstructure, the excess because the most important thing is the content. This is a theatrical choice which is epic rather than naturalistic.'

While such differences account for and determine, to a certain extent, the appropriation of Fo's texts by British interpreters, there is another element that needs to be taken into account: the foreignness of Fo's work, the fact that it comes from another country. Michael Billington (1983) addressed this issue in his review of the London production of *Can't Pay? Won't Pay!* in its second year at the Criterion Theatre. He argued that the play is funny, but safe for British audiences and wondered if a British playwright attacking the domestic political structure would have been as successful as Fo: 'I just wonder whether he or she would be embraced quite clearly so eagerly by the West End and transformed into a popular hit. Would we, in fact, be quite so ready to turn it into a friend?' What Billington is saying is that Fo's texts can be successfully staged in the West End because they are foreign. Since his work does not directly relate to the target society, it becomes an unusual product that British audiences go and see in the same way as they might look at exotic animals in the zoo. As a consequence, audiences can relate to his work and laugh without feeling threatened by its ideological implications. As will be shown in the next chapter, a distancing strategy emphasising the otherness of Fo's work has often been adopted by his American rewriters.

Furthermore, scholars and theatre practitioners have often questioned West End productions of Fo's plays arguing against the validity of political theatre when it is staged in mainstream venues. McGrath's opposition to the establishment is one of the foundations of his working-class theatre manifesto and of his personal experience as a theatre professional (McGrath, 1981). In his view, writing plays for bourgeois theatres such as the National Theatre, the Royal Shakespeare or West

End theatres, or presenting them on those stages would negate the validity of any political commitment. The popular theatre advocated by McGrath is a revolutionary form of theatre aimed at the abolition of capitalism and classes. Clive Barker argues that when looking at political theatre, the question 'Can any effective political theatre be constructed and exist within a government system?' needs to be asked (Barker, 1992: 37). He also claims that most political theatre in Western Europe is a theatre of bourgeois extraction, which embodies the interests of the middle class, as opposed to Piscator's theatre supporting the revolution.

Needless to say, the above mentioned scholars' perspective is based on an old-fashioned Marxist ideology, a transgressive approach that, as previously argued, was out of date by the 1980s and that becomes even more so in the post cold-war era of the 21st century. Fo's view about the fact that his plays are performed in mainstream theatres is instead quite different. When, during the 1984 press conference in New York, Fo was asked his opinion, he replied as follows:

> Sono stato rappresentato nei teatri più istituzionali del mondo, ma le peggiori messe in scena dei miei lavori, le ho viste proprio nelle sale più cosiddette rivoluzionarie. Ciò che conta infatti è la coerenza, il rispetto della chiave ideologica. D'altra parte anche Brecht è stato rappresentato a Broadway e nessuno del Berliner Ensemble ha mai protestato.[11]

In a telephone interview in February 2000, he explained that, after being staged in alternative venues, his work is taken to mainstream theatres, in the London West End or on Broadway, simply because it is successful. While Fo accepts and even appreciates the fact that his works may be staged in mainstream theatres, given the success they usually achieve (with the exception of the Broadway fiasco), the theatrical, financial and cultural constraints affecting the translation of theatre texts nevertheless increase the risks of transforming politically committed theatre into comforting mainstream plays.

This process becomes particularly evident in the transfer of Fo's work from Italian into English and leads us to the most important aspect of its British acculturation. What happens is that Fo's revolutionary theatre is reduced to theatre with a political content. As Holderness (1992) argues, a politics of content is not effective if its form and function reinforce the dominant ideology. On the contrary a theatre which questions the ideological mechanisms of society and stimulates the spectator to think critically, as Fo's theatre does in Italy, is politically more progressive. Taken out of its Italian context, the political content of Fo's theatre can be maintained, while its function and efficacy tend to be altered. Thus the theatrical quality of Fo's plays is given priority over its political role. Furthermore,

---

[11] My plays have been staged in the most mainstream theatres around the world, but I have seen the worst productions in the most revolutionary theatres. What counts is coherence, the respect for the ideological perspective. Even Brecht's plays have been staged on Broadway and nobody from the Berliner Ensemble has ever complained about it. (Quoted in Capretti, 1984: 31).

as previously discussed, Fo's foreign identity and cultural remoteness contribute to such manipulation of his texts because they allow domestic producers and receivers to detach themselves from the issues dealt with in his theatre. On the one hand, thanks to prestigious productions on Broadway and London's West End, Fo's work manages to reach an audience that would not otherwise see his plays when staged in fringe theatres. On the other hand, the benefits of reaching new groups of spectators may be defused by the process of manipulation carried out by British rewriters. This becomes clear if we look at how the British image of Fo was constructed and we take into account critics and audiences' expectations when going to see his plays.

Fo is commonly known as a revolutionary left-wing playwright, as the author of subversive farces. Farce is the term most often used by British reviewers to identify Fo's plays, which have been more than once compared to the Marx Brothers' work.[12] But David Hirst argues that 'a distortion' of Fo's work has been presented to British audiences. In his view, in the United Kingdom 'Fo has become a respectable writer in the trendy bourgeois theatre: a fate which he deplores and which he does not deserve' (Hirst, 1989: 16). In his extensive analysis of the British response to Fo's theatre, Mitchell devotes a lot of attention to the results of such distortion (Mitchell, 1999).

One of the factors which has contributed to the process of appropriation of Fo's plays is the transfer of the Belt and Braces production of *Accidental Death of an Anarchist* from the Fringe to the West End in 1980, when it moved to the Wyndham's Theatre. This phenomenon has drawn the attention of a number of scholars and critics who have examined those aspects of British Fo which distinguish him from the Italian Fo. According to Lorch, '*Accidental Death of an Anarchist* has kept its distinction as an Italian play while developing a separate life in its English target culture' (Lorch, 2000: 149). Caroline Tisdall (1980), among others, wrote that the West End success of *Accidental Death* indicated that Fo's career had been subject to 'an Anglicised inversion'. As previously explained, since the late 1960s Fo and Rame distanced themselves from mainstream theatre and stopped performing in bourgeois venues. Instead they devoted their plays to working class problems and performed to crowds of thousands of people in alternative spaces, such as workers' clubs and sport stadiums. As Tisdall argued, staging Fo's plays in London's West End constituted a regression, 'a far cry' from the subversive role that his theatre had in the source culture.

The incredible success of *Accidental Death* in the West End leads us to another issue, that is to say the fact that the above-mentioned socialist groups, such as 7:84, CAST, Belt and Braces, benefited from British government grants. To be more precise, alternative theatre companies were significantly under-subsidised compared with establishment theatres, despite criticisms and protests against the Arts Council's unequal distribution of fundings. Having said that, as Itzin argues,

---

[12] Morley, 1979; Billington, 1979; Hood, 1991.

political theatre groups could have not developed as much as they did without subsidy, which of course represents a fundamental contradiction, given their political aims (Itzin, 1980). Interestingly enough, according to Lorch, the financial benefits of the West End production of *Accidental Death* made the group lose the subsidies from the Arts Council. Paradoxically, it contributed to the financial problems of alternative theatre groups in the United Kingdom because the Belt and Braces production demonstrated that they could support themselves without any government funding (Lorch, 2000). The fact that Belt and Braces asked audiences for donations to support them in view of future funds cutting was criticised by Sheridan Morley precisely for the above-mentioned reason:

> True, the threatened Arts Council cutbacks (by no means yet confirmed) are appalling, but it ill behoves a company having achieved such an anarchically good box-office success to turn round and demand public money for it. Belt & Braces does after all indicate some form of self support. (Morley, 1979)

Despite Morley's claims, the success of *Accidental Death* in financial terms represented a unique experience for Belt and Braces which, together with other political theatre groups, was hugely affected by the government's policy to further reduce subsidy to alternative theatre companies, as it had been announced. In Itzin's words, 'as subsidy had been crucial to the growth of political theatre, so it would be instrumental in its decline' (Itzin, 1980: 339). It was a vicious circle whereby those government subsidies, which had made it possible for political theatre groups to pursue their aims, caused their collapse once they were withdrawn, since no alternative systems of funding had been created.

In this sense Fo and Rame's 'La Comune' distinguishes itself from its British counterparts for its ability to support itself. At this point it might be useful to reflect on the differences between the British and the Italian alternative theatre circuit, as well as on the peculiarity of Fo and Rame's collective. The latter was one among a number of Italian cooperative groups operating in an alternative environment, opposed to that of the mainstream 'teatri stabili', funded repertory theatres. 'La Comune' was created as a private club and therefore spectators who went to see Fo and Rame's performances were at the same time members of the theatre group. The incredibly high number of subscriptions, which was far superior to that of most repertory theatres, allowed 'La Comune' to survive without any state funding. Moreover, the financial autonomy of Fo and Rame's company should not be separated from their commitment to raise funds for a number of social and political causes. As previously explained, in those years Fo and Rame drew thousands of people to their performances while supporting workers and political prisoners in need. The combination of all these elements explains how 'La Comune' differs from British theatre groups, such as Belt and Braces which, despite a similar political commitment, operated on a different scale and achieved different results from Fo and Rame's company.

Let us now look at the path that *Accidental Death* followed once it entered the British theatrical system. The play premiered at Dartington College of Arts in February 1979. After touring Sheffield, Liverpool, Birmingham and Manchester, the production transferred to the Half Moon Theatre in October 1979. The Half Moon was one of the few fringe theatres in London which staged plays dealing with issues relevant to the working class and where Brecht's *Mother Courage* was produced in 1973. Thus, *Accidental Death* was presented in an alternative theatrical environment similar to the one in which Fo himself staged his work. Needless to say, Fo's work, and in particular this play, could not be reproduced in the same terms as it was staged in Italy where each performance was updated to document the unfolding of the Pinelli trial. Fo's British interpreters could not have the impact that Fo had in the source culture and they did not perform to thousands of people, but they shared Fo's political beliefs and performed his work on the fringe. This is as far as the common aspects between the source and the target performance text go, because the play changed radically, even before it transferred to the West End.

The programme for the production at the Half Moon was in a newspaper format, containing articles and photographs taken from the British press about police brutality, such as the murder of a teacher, Blair Peach, by the London police during a demonstration, and political events in Northern Ireland. The Valpreda and Pinelli case and the Italian 'strategy of tension' were also extensively illustrated. Thus spectators were invited to make a connection between the Italian events reported in the show and those familiar to them included in the programme. It is Mitchell's view that the extensive programme 'relegated Fo's arguments to an extra-theatrical context' (Mitchell, 1999: 259). Although one cannot deny the informative value of the newspaper-style programme, the latter appears as a compensation for the shortcomings of the *mise en scène* in which the political and social challenges of Fo's performance text are diminished. As Fo argued, Richards's adaptation created 'an erosion at a satirical level, that is to say the relationship of the tragic to the grotesque, which was the foundation of the original work, in favour of solutions which are exclusively comic' (Fo, 1989a: vi).

As we will also see in the next chapter, the emphasis on the comic elements of Fo's work at the expense of its political value, is a predominant aspect of the appropriation of his theatre not only in the English-speaking world, but in most foreign countries. As Fo made clear when I interviewed him in 2000, presenting an exclusively comic reading of his work constitutes the simplest and least challenging choice that adapters and directors can make when staging his plays. Richards's erosion of the satire of *Accidental Death* is apparent throughout his adaptation, which adheres to the British tradition of music-hall and pantomime, as Mitchell also argues (1999). Most of the alterations and additions made to the play point in that direction. The aggressive, although incompetent policemen of the source text become innocuous stock characters in Richards's production and one of them is even called Inspector Pissani. The threat represented by right-wing insidious policemen, whose ignorance and stubbornness can cost people's lives, as in the case of Pinelli, is reduced through an accumulation of slapstick scenes in the British version. For example, there is a scene in which the *Matto*[13] disguises himself as Captain Marcantonio Piccinni and wears a glass eye, a wooden hand and a wooden leg. In Richards's version the dropping of the eye glass, the coming-apart of the wooden hand and of the leg is considerably prolonged and taken to extremes with the addition of other props, including a parrot. This farcical expedient, which in Fo's text represents a visual deconstruction of power, as Joylynn Wing argues (1990: 148), in Richards's *mise en scène* is reduced to a zany scene. A gag with the Superintendent coming back on stage with a blackjack after having beaten up a suspect, and a number of other purely comic situations portraying harmless police figures, were added by Richards and contributed to the transformation of *Accidental Death* into a play based on slapstick humour and silly jokes as opposed to the political satire of the source text.

Among numerous changes, Richards also included the two different endings of the 1973 and 1974 versions of the play. In the first one the *Matto* tells the policemen that his bomb is real and blows himself up. After the lights go out, the audience hears an explosion and the *Matto* is gone, while the actor playing his part reappears as the real judge, bringing the play back to the beginning. In the 1974 version the *Matto* uses the bomb as a threat in order to escape. Richards incorporated both endings as alternatives and had the *Matto* challenging the journalist to make a decision: either let the policemen go or let them blow up. The *Matto* concluded by addressing the audience: 'Oh Dio! Whichever way it goes, you've got to decide. Goodnight!' (Fo, 1989a: 73). But as Mitchell rightly argues (1999: 263), Fo never presented blowing up the police as a possibility in the play, instead he aimed at emphasising their responsibility for the anarchist's death. The double ending in Richards's version constitutes a significant change since, by presenting a terrorist act as a possible option, it functions as a confirmation of the misleading accusations of supporting terrorism brought against Fo. What appears to be a simple theatrical device aimed at making spectators active participants in the dénouement of the play, becomes also a political statement which inevitably affects the image of Fo. This is particularly significant if we take into account the fact that Fo and Rame were prevented from entering the United States three times in the 1980s precisely because they were accused of terrorist affiliations.

What it is important to stress here is that Richards's production was very successful from its staging at the Half Moon to the West End transfer. In 1979 Tariq Ali in the *Socialist Challenge* commented that *Accidental Death* was the best play he had seen in fifteen years and in his view the Belt and Braces production did 'full justice to Fo's satire'. He particularly praised Alfred Molina's performance as the *Matto* and appreciated the sense of 'camaraderie' created at the Half Moon.

---

[13] The Italian word *Matto* has been translated as 'Maniac' in Richards and Emery's versions, as 'Madman' in Cumming and Supple's version and as 'Fool' in Richard Nelson's American version. Mitchell also claims that Richards's translation of 'Matto' as 'Maniac' was appropriated from his own translation (Mitchell, 1999: 260).

Molina, a British actor of Italian origins, was awarded the *Plays and Players* Most Promising Actor Award in 1980. *Accidental Death* transferred to the Wyndham's Theatre because of Ian Albery's economic interests in producing the play. Albery's hope was that the 'product', in his own terms, would make a profit (quoted in Radin, 1980). While Belt and Braces risked accusations of selling out their ideology by staging a play in the heart of commercial theatre, this represented a unique opportunity to exploit commercial venues to present Fo's work to bourgeois audiences who otherwise would not have had access to his theatre. Richards denied the validity of accusations of ideological sell-out and emphasised the integrity of Belt and Braces' political commitment as testified by the fact that the unemployed could buy tickets at a reduced price. Albery's wish became a reality. The success that the production had at the Half Moon continued in the West End.

According to James Felton (1981), it was 'the envy of theatrical managements: spectacularly cheap to put on and profitable to run'. In his view, the play was successful because in the West End 'there is a market for a kind of comedy which works below the level of the average Whitehall farce. People want to see clowns. And if people want clowns they must certainly be allowed to see clowns. Here endeth the lesson' (ibid.). Fenton's comment appears to confirm that *Accidental Death* had been appropriated to meet target audience's expectations. It is worth noticing that the programme distributed at the Wyndham's Theatre did not include photographs of police violence nor captions such as: 'Policemen or psychos? These uninformed assassins are licensed to attack all sections of the working class', which were part of the programme at the Half Moon. What is fascinating is that, while in his home country Fo's extremist political views conveyed by the play were received with hostility by parties of different political affiliations, including the Italian Communist Party, in the United Kingdom, given that the play's political connotations had been diluted, the response was much less controversial and made it possible for the play to be successful in alternative and mainstream theatres. Like Molina, Richards, who replaced him as the *Matto*, was so successful that he was nominated for the Society of West End Theatres Award.

Despite the ideological compromise involved in the West End transfer and Fo's hostility towards Richards's adaptation to the point where he tried to stop productions based on it, this version of the play was the most commonly used for a number of British productions and was also put on university syllabuses. In other words, it became the authoritative text for a long time. Lorch claims that the play, as adapted by Richards, had 'a niche in British culture of the early 1980s' that was not matched by any other production (Lorch, 2000: 156). This was the result of a number of factors, as shown in the present analysis, such as the fact that the play was turned into a domestic product, a music-hall style comedy, which relied on easy jokes and representations of Italian caricatures, as in the case of the policemen. Richards's adaptation also shared with other British versions of Fo's work an exaggerated number of four-letter words and vulgar terms, which transform Fo's complex and colourful use of language into superficial and easily digestible humour.[14] As Hood (1988) argues, this appears to be a common tendency on which adapter and directors rely, but which is applied without the rigour and precision of Fo's theatrical idiom.[15]

Thus, it is appropriate to say that this production reflects some aspects of the British appropriation of Italian theatre. More precisely, the reading of Fo's play operated by Richards stems from his theatrical acculturation of Fo's theatre. The emphasis given to the comic aspects of *Accidental Death* and the reduction of Italian characters to cliché figures indicates the nature of the theatrical frame of reference for Richards's staging. As Fitzpatrick and Sawczak argue, Richards combined the theatrical frame of the source text, that of political documentary theatre, with that of comedy and therefore 'buffoonery rather than counter-information' became the focus of the production (Fitzpatrick and Sawczak, 1995: 25). According to Gillian Hanna, who made the literal translation of the play, this was a wrong choice. In her opinion, when staging foreign political theatre it is important to downplay its foreign identity to insure that British audiences engage with its content and do not limit themselves at laughing at 'funny foreigners'.[16] This was what the second British professional production of *Accidental Death* tried to avoid.

In January 1991 a new English version of *Accidental Death* by the director Tim Supple and the leading actor Alan Cumming was staged in the United Kingdom. This was a National Theatre Education Department touring production, performed in over thirty British regional theatres. Supple won the *Best Comedy Actor* award for his performance in the show. While the Belt and Braces production opted for an exclusively comic interpretation, in this one the play was interpreted 'through a British filter', as Cumming put it (1991: xxiv). The Anglicisation of the play consisted in adapting the Italian political and cultural connotations of the source text to the target society by setting the play in England. The play was filled with references to British events, such as the Guildford Four, the Birmingham Six and Lord Denning. Cumming and Supple even invited Paul Hill, one of the Guildford Four, to rehearsals to comment on the British elements added to the original. Supple explained his approach in the following way: 'We aim to make it as near to

---

[14] Richards also makes gratuitous use of swear words. For example, when the *Matto* pretends to be a priest sent by the Vatican, Bertozzo does not believe him. In English, Bertozzo threatens everybody with a revolver saying 'You calm down. Against the fucking audience (To audience) Sorry!' (Fo, 1989a: 66) A sentence such as 'Hai finito di prendermi per il sedere' (Fo, 1974: 67) becomes: 'Right you filthy pox-ridden pansy you piss me about one more time and I'll ...!' (Fo, 1989a: 23).

[15] It is interesting to note that Ed Emery's translation represents an exception, as he emphasises in the note preceding his translation: 'I have also, by the way, avoided the over-use of Very Rude Words, which may or may not be characteristic of the constabulary world-wide, but which are not characteristic of Dario Fo' (Fo, 1992a: 124).

[16] Interview with Gillian Hanna, London, June 1998.

the audience's experience as possible, so it is dressed and played as though it is set in Britain, although it is an Italian play' (quoted in Gilbey, 1991).

Supple and Cumming's production took place just after the release of the Guilford Four and while it was touring, the Birmingham Six prosecution was being re-examined. In this sense that production was related to current British political events and one can say that Supple and Cumming tried to recreate the political function of the source text. Their version was rewritten and modified until two days before the show opened, in the same way as Fo and Rame constantly update their work. Some changes were made according to suggestions by Fo, who was present during some rehearsals, such as replacing the anarchist song with the *Internationale* at the end of Act One. Cumming and Supple were eager to emphasise that their version was different from Richards's adaptation because they focused on maintaining the political significance of the play without exaggerating the comedy and avoided caricaturing representations of Italian culture. In other words, Supple and Cumming aimed at making the play relevant to British audiences more in political rather than theatrical terms.

The show received a mixed response. Martin Hoyle (1991) found that this production was not as funny as the one based on Richards's adaptation, while others, like Michael Billington, recognised that it was 'politically more potent' (Billington, 1991). Critical accounts of Supple and Cumming's production testify to the authority that Richards's version had acquired in the United Kingdom given that some critics, like Clare Bayley (1991), commented with assurance about Fo's work by basing their arguments on Richards's version. Similarly Melanie McDonagh (1991), while claiming that 'monstrous liberties have been taken with the original text', gives no specific indication of a direct knowledge of the source text and her assumption appears to be based on a comparison of the 1991 production with Richards's adaptation, rather than with Fo's text, as Mitchell suggests (Mitchell, 1999). One needs to bear in mind that, in the same way as Zeffirelli's productions constituted the only vehicle of access to De Filippo's theatre in the 1970s for many spectators and critics in the United Kingdom, Richards's adaptation of *Accidental Death* represented Fo's theatre for British audiences for a long time. Because it was the first, and very successful production of Fo's play, also broadcast on television by Channel Four on 8 September 1983, it acquired a primary position in the target theatrical system and in the horizon of expectations of spectators and critics, as the above-mentioned reviews show. So when Hilary Hutcheon in her review of the Supple and Cumming's production writes that: 'Something is missing. Cumming and Supple aim to show Italy through a British filter and thus to see both clearly, but there is a distinct absence of fiery machismo and passion here. The English version of *Accidental Death*, by its very nature, simply isn't Italian enough' (Hutcheon, 1991), her perception of the show as not being Italian enough stems from British productions of Italian theatre, such as Richards's staging of *Accidental Death*, relying on caricaturing images of Italy in which machismo and passion function as identifying cultural markers.

Another Fo play, adapted by Bill Colvill and Robert Walker, first staged at the Half Moon in 1978 with the title *We Can't Pay? We Won't Pay!* was revised in 1981 and transferred to the West End as *Can't Pay? Won't Pay!*, where it ran for two years. It was directed by Walker, an experienced director of British alternative theatre who had introduced the work of Peter Handke to the United Kingdom, and had directed British productions of Brecht's work. The play is based on anti-inflation protests occurring in Italy in the 1970s and opens with working-class women who rebel against the rising cost of living by refusing to pay for food bought at a store. The adaptation and the West End success of the show testify, as in the case of *Accidental Death*, to the process of the British appropriation of Fo's work. While the original location, Milan, was kept together with the characters' Italian names, considerable cuts and alterations were made to the play. Both Mitchell and Hirst emphasise the defects of the adaptation. Hirst in particular argues that 'The adaptation's excessive – and imprecise – jokiness in presentation of the police seriously undermines Fo's satire' (Hirst 1989: 96). An example of this was represented by the following music-hall style gag added by Colvill and Walker when the Sergeant arrives on stage:

> *Sergeant appears in window at rear, clinging to swaying drainpipe.*
> Sergeant: Oi (*Giovanni, back to window, shoots arms up*)
> Giovanni: O my good God. I'll get shot in the back resisting arrest. (*Sergeant sways across window again.*)
> Sergeant: Oi
> Giovanni: All right, all right. I'll come quietly. (*Sergeant sways back into view*)
> Sergeant: Oi. You Desist. (*He hooks a foot over window-sill*)
> Giovanni: Desist? Desist? I am desisting, aren't I? What more can I desist?
> Sergeant: Does this flat belong to you?
> Giovanni: Yes.
> Sergeant: I order you to assist me.
> Giovanni: Oh, yeah? How? Beat myself up? Punch myself in the nuts?
> Sergeant: Help!
> Giovanni: Stop mucking about.
> Sergeant: Help!
> Giovanni: What a sense of humour. (*Now Giovanni turns around and sees policeman clinging to drainpipe with foot in saucepan on windowsill*) I don't believe it. What are you playing at?
> Sergeant: Help! EEEEK!
> Giovanni: (Out front) Now that's the law all over. Popping round to do you over they can't come in the door like everyone else. No: door's not good enough for the like of them. Oh no. Tell you what, there was this copper who wanted to get a new pair of boots – this'll kill you –
> Sergeant: No. It'll kill me. HELP!
> Giovanni: Don't interrupt. Oh sorry.
> Sergeant: Get me out of this.
> Giovanni: What's wrong with the door?
> Sergeant: Get me out of this.
> Giovanni: What are you doing there?

Sergeant: It's a search.
Giovanni: Oh, yeah? Find anything?
Sergeant: We're searching your flat.
Giovanni: Oh, yeah? Got a warrant?
Sergeant: IF YOU DON'T GET ME–
Giovanni: All right. All right. Don't get shirty. (*Ad libs*)
Sergeant drops onto balcony and comes through French windows. Goes up behind Giovanni)
Giovanni: (*Not realising who he's talking to*) There's a copper hanging out of the window.
Sergeant: Oh really?
Giovanni: He wants to come in.
Sergeant: Why doesn't he use the door?
Giovanni: (*Realising*) What do you want?
Sergeant: It's a search.
(Fo, 1994b: 17-18)

The second act of the play was considerably reduced. For example, the women's battle against the police at the end of the play was cut and the final song, expressing the characters' hope for a better world, free of corruption and crime, was replaced by a song conveying stereotypical images of Italian women, *Sebben che siamo donne*. Most important of all, as Hirst argues (1989: 105), the Colvill-Walker adaptation turned a political play addressing real working class needs into a bourgeois play revolving around the four main characters' sentimental relationships.

When the Half Moon production was re-mounted at the Criterion, a pink and blue set was used, based on an image of Neapolitan ice cream. Rather than aiming at creating a working class environment, the set was designed to convey the Italianness of the show symbolised by the colours of the ice-cream. Although the phrasing of the English title became quite popular and was used as a slogan in demonstrations against Mrs. Thatcher's poll tax, a number of British productions of the play appear to confirm the predominance of the entertainment value of Fo's play at the expense of its political relevance.

But Billington praised Walker's production for bringing Fo's subversive farce to the West End:

Ironic to hear a West End audience cheering on a play that preaches anarchy, theft, class-war, and bopping the fuzz. But I find it heartening that a subversive Italian farce like *Can't Pay, Won't Pay* has made it from the left-wing ghettoes into the capitalist citadel. Clearly manager Ian Albery has decided it is better to have the Fo within that the enemy without. (...) The danger is, of course, that a pretty well-fed London audience that has not had to face, as yet, 41 per cent inflation, treats it all as a romp and swallows the sugar without the pill. (Billington, 1981)

The tone is different from that of Hirst writing about 'a distortion' of Fo's theatre. While acknowledging the contrast between Fo's work and the environment in which the latter is performed, 'the capitalist citadel', Billington appreciates the fact that conservative audiences like West End theatre-goers have the opportunity to see a provocative play like *Can't Pay? Won't Pay!* But the risk that middle-class spectators might treat the play simply as a funny Italian comedy cannot be ignored, as previously argued. As Mitchell puts it, 'The universal nature of the play's theme, together with its smooth proficiency as an almost well-made farce, made it easier for West End audiences to enjoy the comedy without pondering unduly its radical political message of appropriation' (Mitchell, 1999: 253).

Billington wrote another review in 1983 which indicates the consequences of the process of acculturation of Fo's work in the United Kingdom. He posed a number of questions and wondered among other things whether the farce and the politics in Fo's play were well integrated. He argued that what Fo does in the play is to take a classic comic situation, i.e. the hiding of a growing number of goods and then 'grafts on to it a number of political homilies'. Billington gives an example of a scene where the action stops to let one of the female protagonists preach on the lack of support from the Communist Party. In Billington's opinion, that political homily had nothing to do with the action of the play. His view that Fo's political themes are external additions to the dynamics of his plays is more a result of the Anglicisation of Fo's theatre rather than an inherent quality of his work. On the contrary, Fo's theatre always stems from political events and social issues, which constitute an integral aspect of his scripts and are thoroughly assimilated in a theatrical form to entertain and critically stimulate his audience at the same time. Rame's emphasis on the technical precision of Fo's texts makes this clear:

> He invents dialogue on a paradoxical or a real situation and goes on from there by virtue of some kind of natural, geometric logic, inventing conflicts that find their solutions in one gag after the another in correspondence with a parallel political theme, a political theme which must be clear and didactic. You are moved and you laugh, but above all you are made to think, realise and develop your understanding of everyday events that had before escaped your attention. (Rame, 1994: xxix)

After two successful productions in the West End, four pieces (*Medea, A Woman Alone, Waking Up* and *The Same Old Story*) from *Tutta casa, letto e chiesa*, first entitled *Female Parts*, later changed to *One Woman Plays*, were staged at the National Theatre, Cottesloe in 1981. The National Theatre production pushed even further the assimilation of his work into British mainstream theatre. The play was translated by Margaret Kunzle, adapted by Olwen Wymark, a fringe playwright, and directed by Michael Bodganov. Yvonne Bryceland performed the monologues. One of the pieces was Fo and Rame's rewriting of the Greek *Medea*, in which the protagonist speaks a dialect from central Italy. In the source text her language differentiates her from the protagonist of Euripides's tragedy, but the same cannot be said for the adaptation, whose standard English did not indicate the popular origins of Fo and Rame's Medea. This language difficulty, together with the adapter's decision to cut the introduction to the piece, affected critical interpretations. In the introduction we learn that the story of *Medea* is not about revenge or jealousy, but it is about a woman who has taken a moral stand and has refused to comply with a society dominated by men. As a result, Irving Wardle, writing for *The Times*, assumed that the monologue was 'a feminist justification for child slaughter' (Wardle, 1981).

Another piece, *Waking Up* is about the frustrations of a working-class wife trying to cope with her responsibilities as a mother and a worker in a factory. But Wymark's adaptation failed to convey the working-class status of the protagonist and the language used did not manage to express her anger and disillusionment. In another monologue, *A Woman Alone*, a wife talks about her experience as a segregated woman locked up at home by her husband. James Fenton commented that Yvonne Bryceland's performance convinced the audience that the protagonist is superficial and he came to the conclusion that 'The plight of Woman comes to seem nothing more than her own silly fault' (Fenton, 1981). Fenton's comment indicates that Bryceland's interpretation turned a provocative critique of male power over women into an account of a stupid woman. It also raises the previously mentioned issue of the impact of naturalist acting training of English-speaking actors when they perform Fo and Rame's plays, which similarly characterises American productions of their theatre, as will be shown in the next chapter. Furthermore, it is interesting to note that in this production a naturalist setting for both *A Woman Alone* and *Waking Up* replaced the bare stage of Rame's performances in Italy. All these factors, the language of the adaptation, Bryceland's interpretation and the choice of the setting, diminished the political significance of the pieces. In this sense the National Theatre production contributed to the British transformation of Fo and Rame's work. Wardle's comment that Fo and Rame's theatre focuses on women's condition in Italy, which he identifies as the country of origin of the word 'machismo', shows a tendency to emphasise the foreignness of Fo and Rame's work. As previously argued, this is a way of distancing the receiving culture from the source culture and dismissing the provocative content of Fo and Rame's plays by categorising them as Italian.

One production that deserves attention for presenting provocative monologues from *Tutta casa, letto e chiesa*, excluded from the National Theatre production, is *The Fourth Wall* staged by Monstrous Regiment, at the Drill Hall in London in 1983. Two pieces included in this show were *I'm Ulrike Screaming* and *It Happened Tomorrow*. These monologues narrate the story of Ulrike Meinhof and Irmgard Moeller, members of the Red Army Fraction, a German left-wing terrorist organisation. The first was found dead in the Stammheim prison in Munich, while the second survived serious injuries reported as a suicide attempt. The selection of such disturbing monologues as a result of Monstrous Regiment's feminist commitment represented a departure from the image of Fo and Rame's theatre conveyed by the National Theatre production. Moreover, Gillian Hanna's approach to their work distinguished the *mise en scène* of *The Fourth Wall* from other British stagings, such as Richards's production of *Accidental Death* and Walker's production of *Can't Pay? Won't Pay!* As she argues in the introduction to her translations, Hanna believes in the importance of staging Fo and Rame's plays without adopting stereotypical representations of Italians:

> The point is particularly tricky when dealing with the comic plays, and leads to a crucial issue: whether to leave the character in an Italian context or move her to a place which the audience is likely to recognise more immediately, and where there is a greater chance of them laughing *with* the character rather than *at* her. (Rame and Fo, 1991: xvii)

In this respect, both the Monstrous Regiment production of *The Fourth Wall* and Supple and Cumming's adaptation of *Accidental Death* represent two exceptions to exclusively comic readings of Fo and Rame's plays, as in the case of the 1992 West End production of *The Pope and the Witch*, at the Comedy Theatre. But before looking at this staging as the latest example of the Anglicisation of Fo and Rame's work, it is worth taking into account their live performances in London in 1983 and 1984.

In May 1983 Fo performed *Mistero Buffo* and Rame performed *Tutta casa, letto e chiesa* at the Riverside Studios, London, and they held workshops with British theatre professionals. Fo's prologues to the *Mistero Buffo* pieces were translated on stage by Stuart Hood, while during Fo and Rame's performances English supertitles were projected. Fo and Rame's shows received public acclaim and sold out during the three week run. It is interesting to note that, in commenting on Fo's unique abilities, some British critics tried to classify him by comparing him with well-known performers. For example, Jim Hiley (1983) argued that 'It's as if Terry Wogan had suddenly acquired the technique of Marcel Marceau, the charisma of Richard Pryor, the intellectualism of Jonathan Miller and the politics of Ken Livingstone.' Brian Glanville (1983) compared Fo's walk to John Cleese's walks and argued that 'Like Roy Hudd he may crack a difficult joke and pretend that one part of the audience has got it, the joke and the other hasn't.' Fo and Rame returned to the Riverside Studios in January 1984 for the Dario Fo/Franca Rame Theatre Project which consisted of a week of events, including rehearsed readings of Fo and Rame's plays, some of which had never been performed in the United Kingdom, like *I Don't Move, I Don't Scream, My Voice is Gone*, *The Mother* and *Michele Lu Lanzone*, and monologues by English women playwrights, such as Pam Gems and Michelene Wandor. The project included a forum on British political theatre and feminism. This was a further opportunity for reciprocal exchange between British and Italian theatre practitioners. The critical recognition given to their theatre is testified to by Irving Wardle's comment in *The Times*: 'Dario Fo's brief season at Riverside last spring was a revelation comparable to London's first sight of the Berliner Ensemble, and it is good news that this event is still bearing fruit' (Wardle, 1984). Fo and Rame also performed monologues from *Mistero Buffo* and *Tutta casa, letto e chiesa* at the Edinburgh Fringe Festival in 1984 and 1986.

Thus, the period between 1983 and 1986 constitutes a window through which

British audiences, critics and theatre professionals had direct access to Fo and Rame's work. Most important of all, this was an opportunity for the target society to experience Fo and Rame's acting style and their 'epic' theatre, as opposed to British stagings of their plays informed by a naturalist approach or by music-hall. This was achieved not only through their performances, but also through their workshops, in which Fo and Rame discussed their theatre experiences and techniques. According to Hanna, the impact of Rame's presence was testified to by the fact that some of her monologues became part of the repertoire of British actresses who took part in the Dario Fo/Franca Rame Theatre Project.[17] But one cannot underestimate the fact that Fo and Rame's performances and workshops had by definition a more limited reach – both in terms of time and space, given the small number of seats at the Riverside Studios – than the long lasting West End productions of their plays preceding and following their visits to the United Kingdom.

The British image of Fo and Rame was in fact reinforced by the West End productions of *Trumpets and Raspberries* and *The Pope and the Witch*. Benedict Nightingale's review of *Trumpets and Raspberries* confirms this:

> There's something suspicious about a Fo phenomenon that is rapidly becoming a Fo flow. Here's a playwright whom respectable Communist parties have attacked for leaning dangerously far to the Left ... and here he is seeking his third consecutive commercial triumph with his third consecutive laugh-riot in the traditional centre of British bourgeois entertainment. (Nightingale, 1984)

Once again British readers and audiences were reminded of the contrast between the role of Fo's work in his home country and the commercial success of British productions of his plays in the West End. Nightingale also expressed his hope that despite the fact that Fo's theatre had been considerably altered and transformed into a profitable business, theatre-goers would be able to relate to it on a social and political level, besides enjoying themselves. But the foreignness of the political events on which the play was based, together with the comic emphasis of the *mise en scène*, seem to preclude such a response. *Trumpets and Raspberries* is about the kidnapping of the Christian Democrat leader, Aldo Moro, former Italian Prime Minister. More precisely, the play revolves around a case of mistaken identity between Antonio, a Fiat worker and the Fiat boss Gianni Agnelli, the most powerful Italian businessman. The latter is disfigured in a car accident when terrorists try to kidnap him, undergoes plastic surgery and is then mistaken for Antonio. Terrorism and the kidnapping of Moro were central and controversial issues in the Italian political context of the time. As Valentini argued (1981), Fo was the only one writing about such disturbing events dominating Italian politics. Needless to say, British audiences had only a limited knowledge, if any, of these events and of Agnelli's predominant role, which made the play innocuous, even

---

[17] Interview with Gillian Hanna, London, June 1998.

meaningless, as Hirst (1989) argues. Furthermore, the production was an opportunity for Griff Rhys Jones to display his abilities as a comedian. Jones was best known for radio and television light entertainment, particularly for comedy shows such as *Not the Nine O'clock News*. His performance, as Agnelli and Antonio Berardi, pushed the play even more in the direction of a farce without any subversive implications, as John Barber argued in the *Daily Telegraph*:

> An artless dish, resembling a high-flavoured Italian risotto drowned in homely English ketchup, "Trumpets and Raspberries" at the Phoenix, is less a play than a jolly excuse for Griff Rhys Jones to cross his eyes, pull funny faces and function generally as the avuncular life of a rather slow party. (Barber, 1984)

But despite that, this production was 'likely to win Fo new friends', as Billington put it (Billington, 1984).

The 1992 production of *The Pope and the Witch* represents the latest staging of a Fo play in the land of British mainstream theatre, but it is important to consider that *The Pope and the Witch*, together with other plays, bears the mark of changed social and political circumstances in Italy which affected Fo and Rame's theatre. The play, in fact, was staged in 1989 when the working class movement was in decline. Joseph Farrell, using colours to identify different phases in Fo's theatrical career, argues that the 'red' period of the late 1960s and 1970s was followed by 'a rose mood', because of Fo and Rame's feminist pieces, such as *Tutta casa, letto e chiesa* (Farrell, 2000: 4), while, in his political biography of Fo, Behan defines this as 'the downturn period' (Behan, 2000: 111). Given that by the late 1970s the workers' struggle was going through a crisis, those issues which had been the focus of Fo and Rame's theatre became irrelevant and detached from the Italian political context of the time. This is why Fo and Rame's theatre started to deal with other political and social issues, such as the position of women in society and the drug problem, as in the case of *The Pope and The Witch*. This also explains why Fo and Rame started to perform in traditional theatres again. They aimed at provoking and making traditional theatre audiences aware of current political and social issues. In Behan's view, 'Fo and Rame had not lost their political and social commitment, they were simply living through times very different to those of the 1970s' (Behan, 2000: 132). In other words, the shift in their theatre was determined by and was parallel to changing social and political circumstances.

When *The Pope and the Witch* was staged in Italy, as Anna Bandettini argues, critics and audiences were at the same time looking forward to and feared the première of the play. The performance was considered to be challenging on a number of levels:

> Un ritorno alle scene quello dei due artisti ovviamente atteso ma anche temuto perché questo nuovo spettacolo sembra toccare tutte in una volta le corde più sensibili della nostra attualità politica, sociale e religiosa. ... Lo spettacolo è ironico, allegro, talvolta

spiazzante, giocato volutamente sui ritmi della commedia, ma le sue conclusioni sono serie, anzi problematiche. (Bandettini, 1989)[18]

The above review seems to indicate that Fo and Rame's theatre continued to be politically relevant, although one should not underestimate the fact that it was functioning in a different context from that of the 1970s and addressing a different kind of audience.

The 1992 British production was based on an adaptation by Andy de la Tour from Ed Emery's literal translation. De la Tour had played the part of the Superintendent in Richards's production of *Accidental Death*. This is why he was approached by the West Yorkshire Playhouse to do the adaptation of *The Pope and the Witch*, as he explains in a programme note. His sister, Frances, who had performed in the 1978 Half Moon production of *Can't Pay? Won't Pay!* played the role of the Witch. De la Tour justified his approach to the play as follows: 'Here was a wonderful satire about the Catholic Church written for a mainly Catholic audience that had to make sense to a mainly non-Catholic British audience. ... Of necessity I had to cut out some references to Catholic individuals and organisations well-known in Italy but not elsewhere' (de la Tour, 1992). Like any translator or adapter, for de la Tour the challenge involved in adapting the play was to make it relevant for British audiences, hence the need to cut references to the Catholic Church that would not be understood in the United Kingdom. But, as he explained, he had an interest in one specific aspect of the play: 'I was particularly interested, though, in expanding the theme touched on in the play concerning alleged Vatican City corruption and the controversial death of the last Pope, John Paul the First' (de la Tour, 1992).

For this reason, he expanded the source text references to the Banco Ambrosiano scandal and the case of the Italian banker Roberto Calvi, found hanging under Blackfriars Bridge in London a few years earlier. He invented a new character, Cardinal Schillaci – Schillaci being an Italian football player – 'to embody the corrupt and violent side of Vatican city politics in the hope of making this side of the play more accessible', as he puts it (de la Tour, 1992). The Cardinal, who spoke with an exaggerated Bronx accent, made explicit references to the Mafia connections of the Church. De la Tour changed all the characters' names to the names of football players from the 1990 Italian World Cup football team. He also added a football chant and Tom Lehrer's cabaret song, *Vatican Rag*, but both of these additions were criticised in the press for being external to the dynamics of the play.[19] Fo did not approve of the football names and requested a change of the first letters of all the characters' names in the translation published by Methuen. Fo

---

[18] 'The two artists' return to the stage has been expected but also feared because this show touches on all the most sensitive chords of our current political, social and religious context. ... The show is ironic, cheerful, at times provocative, purposely played with comic rhythms, but its conclusions are serious, or rather problematic.'

[19] See Coveney, 1992; Gross, 1992.

voiced his criticism of this production for presenting stereotyped images of Italians in an interview with Martin Hoyle (Hoyle, 1992).

Given the above-mentioned additions and alterations, de la Tour's adaptation appears to have followed a pattern similar to Richards's staging in that it similarly relied on the use of stage caricatures of Italians. Furthermore, by giving comic emphasis to the character of the Pope and to the Vatican's corruption and connection with the Mafia, his adaptation shifted the focus of the play. As Fo and Rame argued in an interview with Albert Hunt, the play's principal theme is the use of drugs and the approach of the Italian government towards drug addicts, who are treated as criminals (Hunt, 1991). Fo and Rame's way of approaching the subject was to select a politically important character and then create a conflict within this character to show how young heroin addicts are turned into scapegoats by the Italian government. The Pope was chosen because of his role as an ideological leader. In the play he passes from being a repressor to being a heroin addict by accident and finds himself experiencing the same repression that drug addicts have to face. De la Tour's reading of the source text and his agenda gave priority to the Vatican's corruption, while downplaying the issue of the government responsibility for drug addicts.

The extent to which de la Tour's adaptation of the play might have affected the response of target audiences and critics is indicated by Hunt's own comment following the above-mentioned interview with Fo and Rame:

> My problem is that I'm finding hard to relate this account of what the play is about to the show I'd seen the previous night. ... Watching *The Pope and the Witch* I couldn't help feeling that Dario Fo was a lot more interested in the Pope than in the drug laws. (quoted in Hunt, 1991)

Hunt's reaction to the play shows that the image of Fo's work presented by de la Tour's production of *The Pope and the Witch* acquires a certain validity for the target society. As shown in the course of this analysis, critics often fall into the trap of perceiving translators' choices as the choices of the foreign writer without questioning the former's interpretation of the source text and without knowing the foreign text. This was particularly evident in some critical accounts of this production. John Gross attributed the main responsibilities for the failure of *The Pope and the Witch* to Fo and suggested that if the show made the audience realise that *Can't Pay? Won't Pay!* and *Accidental Death* were overrated, it had served its purpose (Gross, 1992). Similarly Charles Spencer argued that Fo's reputation in the United Kingdom was ludicrously inflated, although he attributed some responsibility for this particular production to de la Tour, whom he defined as 'one of the unfunniest comedians on the alternative cabaret circuit' (Spencer, 1992). It is clear that such a response was the result of de la Tour's strategy, which applied to a play like *The Pope and the Witch*, differing from previous plays for the above-mentioned reasons, magnified the political shift in Fo and Rame's work, thus affecting their image even further. It is also interesting to note that these reactions contrast with the positive response to previous stagings, such as Richards's production of *Accidental Death* and Walker's version of *Can't Pay? Won't Pay!*, which similarly emphasised the slapstick humour of Fo's plays and conveyed stereotypical images of Italians. Such responses might indicate that stagings informed by this approach were not as popular as they had been in previous years because of a change in critical and public reception.[20]

To conclude, the productions analysed in this chapter testify to a bourgeois transformation, a commercialisation of Fo's theatre, as opposed to its revolutionary nature in the source culture. We have seen how the image of Fo constructed by his British rewriters through translations and productions of his plays affected audience perceptions. Particularly in the 1970s and 1980s, when going to see a Fo play, British audiences expected to see hilarious and innocuous farces, conforming to the style of slapstick, music-hall and, to different extents, to caricaturing stage representations of Italians. Despite the differences between the British and American cultural and theatrical systems, the process of Anglicisation of Fo's theatre shares some common aspects with the American appropriation of his work, as will be shown in the next chapter.

---

[20] Such shift in the response to Fo's plays would also appear to parallel the success achieved by 1990s British stagings of Luigi Pirandello and Eduardo De Filippo's work, such as the Almeida production of *Naked* and Peter Hall's staging of *Filumena*, which acculturated those plays to make them accessible to target audiences, rather than emphasising their Italianness.

Figure 1 The Eureka Theatre production of *Accidental Death of an Anarchist*

Figure 2 Harriet Haris, Geoff Hoyle, John Geisz, Remo Airaldi, and John Bottoms in the American Repertory Theatre production of *Archangels Don't Play Pinball*

Figure 3 The West Yorkshire Playhouse production of *The Pope and the Witch*.

Figure 4 Thomas Derrah in the title role of *Johan Padan and the Discovery of the Americas*, which received its American première at the ART

Figure 5 Further scene from *Johan Padan and the Discovery of the Americas*.

Figure 6 The Dallas Theater production of *Accidental Death of an Anarchist*

Figure 7 Further scene from *Accidental Death of an Anarchist*

Figure 8 The Borderline production of *Mistero Buffo*

Figure 9 Further scene from *Mistero Buffo*

Figure 10 Fo performing *Mistero Buffo* at Wesleyan Center for the Arts

Chapter 4

Fo and Rame on the American Stage

The American response to Fo and Rame's theatre reveals some elements in common with the British reception. A tendency to highlight the comic aspects of their theatre against its political function similarly characterises a large number of American stagings. As a result the provocative Italian Fo and Rame are turned into Americanised bourgeois playwrights, as Alisa Salomon argues (1983a: 65). The role of Fo and Rame's American adapters, such as Ron Davis and his several productions of *We Won't Pay! We Won't Pay!* will be given particular attention. It will also be argued that the nature of political theatre and actor training in the United States has affected the American *mises en scène* of Fo and Rame's work. The final part of the chapter will focus on regional productions which are an exception to the Americanising approach.

There is one aspect that is unique to the history of Fo and Rame in the United States, and that is the denial of an American visa on three occasions. The American and the Italian press devoted a lot of attention to what was identified as the 'Fo case'. After having been prevented from entering the United States in 1980, 1983 and 1984, Fo and Rame were finally allowed into the country just for the opening of *Accidental Death of an Anarchist* on Broadway.[1] The show, which was nevertheless a fiasco in New York, constitutes a fascinating case study demonstrating the impact of the American press, economic factors and audiences' expectations on the destiny of theatrical shows. When Fo and Rame came back to the United States to perform in 1986, they were received with public acclaim, as will be shown later.[2]

In an interview with Sergio Parini, Fo argued that *Accidental Death of an Anarchist* was the first Italian play to be performed in a Broadway theatre, since

---

[1] The play, adapted by Richard Nelson from a translation by Suzanne Cowan and directed by Douglas Wager, opened at the Belasco Theater on 15 November 1984. This was a transfer of the Arena Theatre Company production which had been staged at the Kreeger Theater in Washington DC, from 3 February to 18 March 1984.

[2] Fo and Rame performed *Mistero Buffo* and *Tutto casa, letto e chiesa*, from 30 April to 20 June 1986, at the American Repertory Theatre (ART) in Cambridge, Massachusetts, the Yale Repertory Theatre in New Haven, Connecticut, the Joyce Theatre in New York, the Kennedy Center for Performing Arts in Washington DC and in Baltimore during the International Festival. They also came back to the United States when Ron Jenkins's translation of *Archangels Don't Play Pinball* was staged in 1987 at the American Repertory Theatre and directed by Fo, who also rewrote the play inserting references to American political events.

plays by Luigi Pirandello, Eduardo De Filippo and others by Fo had been put on off and off-off-Broadway, but not on Broadway. Fo also emphasised what he saw as the American xenophobic approach to foreign theatre: 'Tutte le opere europee presentate recentemente a New York sono state pesantemente aggredite da critici e intellettuali' (Parini, 1984: 25).[3] An insular attitude towards foreign theatre, and in particular Italian theatre, is one among a series of common aspects between the United States and the United Kingdom. As previously indicated, in David Hirst's (1983) and Clive Barker's view (1981), the limited knowledge of Italian theatre in the United Kingdom is related to the insular nature of British theatre. American scholars and critics complain about the isolationism of their own theatre as often as their British colleagues do. Clives Barnes in a review of the 1980-1981 New York production of *We Won't Pay! We Won't Pay!* at the Chelsea Theatre argued that 'Dramatically speaking, we live in an isolationist world. This isolationism runs through the English-speaking theater, and is common in Britain as in the United States. We are, to quite a large part, cut off from contemporary drama' (Barnes, 1980: 15). According to Charles Mann, the fact that this production was the first opportunity for American audiences to see a Fo play revealed 'the abysmal state' of American political theatre (1980: 114). A few years later, when Fo was still not allowed into the country, Joel Schechter defined him as the most influential political playwright since Brecht and lamented the limited knowledge of his work in the United States, given that over thirty of his plays had not been translated nor staged. In Schechter's view, the denial of a visa to Fo and Rame revealed 'cultural impoverishment and political biases that are peculiarly American' (Schechter, 1984: 112).

Another main cause of the limited knowledge of Fo's work in the United States, in Schechter's opinion, is the American attitude towards political theatre combined with the financial risks involved. As Schechter argues, the fact that theatre professionals are 'box office conscious ... militates against strong, political satire and politically biased presentations that might unsettle the settled, paying sector of the public' (Schechter, 1984: 113). This is particularly true in New York where mounting a production can cost a fortune. *Accidental Death of an Anarchist*, for example, cost about half a million dollars. Thus theatre companies are unwilling to take risks and stage unknown political plays, the more so if they are foreign. In his review of the New York staging of *We Won't Pay! We Won't Pay!*, Charles Mann commented on the obstacles facing anybody wanting to stage Fo's work:

> Bringing *We Won't Pay* to life here has not been easy. The entire theatre system in New York is skewed against political works, not so much because of a coherent bias against pinko plays, but as a systematic eschewal of intellectual content. Part of this is traceable

---

[3] 'All European plays recently staged in New York have been strongly attacked by critics and intellectuals.'

to what Richard Hofstadter called "the national disrespect for the mind", and part is because producers and actors are scared of "offending" people. (Mann, 1980: 114)

Mann emphasises the hostility against political theatre, specifying that New York theatre is not so much against left-wing plays, rather against anything intellectually engaging. This justification appears to be over-simplistic, despite the fact that there is some truth in it. It will be demonstrated how the importance of a politically correct approach appears to inform American stagings of Fo's plays characterised by a distancing strategy as a 'safe' choice to engage domestic audiences. Rather than stimulating or provoking theatre-goers, the easiest and most common option is to stage plays which do not threaten anybody because they take place somewhere else. What I would like to question here is the assumption that the political nature of Fo's plays represents the main obstacle to the staging of his work in the United States. In other words, saying that Fo's work is hard to present to American audiences because they are not accustomed to seeing political plays is only true to a certain extent. But before we look at how Fo's work is acculturated in Davis's productions, we need to define what political theatre means in the American context.

Political theatre in the United States is by and large identified with agitational and didactic theatre, such as agit-prop. One of the most important examples of political theatre in the United States was the Federal Theatre Project (FTP), which was a result of Franklin Delano Roosevelt's New Deal. The FTP was created in 1935 and it had two main aims: to preserve the talents of unemployed actors, directors, and to bring theatre to those Americans who did not have access to commercial theatre. Among other things, the FTP staged the so-called Living newspaper, a new dramatic form, a documentary aimed at informing the audience about the main aspects of a social problem, and encouraging them to take initiatives to solve it. They focused on a variety of social issues such as housing, health care, cooperatives, natural resources, labour unions. Living Newspapers were extremely successful and reached audiences of thousands all over the United States.[4] For the purpose of this analysis, it is important to bear in mind that, because of the impact of the FTP, political theatre in the United States meant agit-prop, Living Newspapers, theatre dealing with social and political issues on an unprecedented scale.

An important group of the time was the Group Theatre, whose work was based on the acting style of Stanislavsky and the Moscow Art Theatre. Harold Clurman, one of the founders of the group, claimed in 1934 that they would 'do more socially conscious plays than any other theatre functioning' (Clurman, 1945: 127). In January 1935 the Group Theatre staged Clifford Odets's *Waiting for Lefty*, a play about the 1934 strike of New York taxi drivers. It soon became very popular and was part of the repertoire of most Workers' Theatre Groups in the United

---

[4] On the history of the FTP see also the 1999 film *The Cradle Will Rock*, directed by Tim Robbins.

States and Western Europe. The play received numerous awards, but was also closed down in Boston and New Haven. Odets's Marxism and Communism were so emphasised in the press that he was seen as a central figure of the so-called Left Movement in the theatre.[5]

Then in the 1960s, as similarly occurred in the United Kingdom, social upheaval gave rise to an alternative theatre and several groups focused on political issues, often advocating social change. Among these there was the Living Theatre, founded by Julian Beck and Judith Malina. The identifying features of their work were audience confrontation and participation, a breaking down of the separation between stage and auditorium, performing without a text and focusing on real time and place. Theodore Shank suggests that 'some of their work can be considered *political theatre* in that it was concerned with social and economic problems' (Shank, 1982: 3), thus confirming that political theatre continued to be equated with socially relevant theatre. The San Francisco Mime Troupe, founded by Ron Davis, was a political theatre group which attacked America's establishment, focusing on current social and political problems and allowing an active participation of their audiences during their shows, mainly performed in parks in San Francisco. Joan Holden believes that change in society comes from people who are uncomfortable, who are in a difficult position and argues: 'It is the objective of the Mime Troupe to help those who do not benefit from the system to understand what is in their self-interest and to see that change is possible' (Holden, 1969: 415). After more than thirty years of activity, they continue to advocate social change and to support mass movements against militarism, sexism and racism.

El Teatro Campesino and The Bread and Puppet Theatre were two other important exponents of American political theatre. The former, founded in Delano by Luis Valdez in 1965, focused on issues relevant to farm workers and their satire was directed at farm owners. El Teatro Campesino performed *actos*, one-act agit-prop plays, which had to be brief to get ideas across quickly during rallies and which were based on slapstick. They took the Mexican comedian Cantinflas as a model, together with Brecht and the San Francisco Mime Troupe. In the Campesino actos, as in the work of the Mime Troupe, figures of authority, like land owners, generals and politicians, are turned into buffoons. The Bread and Puppet Theatre, founded in 1962 by Peter Schumann, was based in Vermont where it held its annual circus festival and is still active today. It used to tour all over the United States, mainly using puppets, distorting and exaggerating politics, and involving spectators in the show as much as possible. Anti-militarism is also one of the identifying marks of its work. Like the San Francisco Mime Troupe, it continues to perform all over the United States.

One of the most vital New York political theatre companies was Richard Schechner's the Performance Group, a theatre collective which performed in its

---

[5] See Samuel et al., 1985.

own space, the Performance Garage. In 1975 Spalding Gray and Elizabeth Le Compte, members of the Performance Group, started to develop their own performances and created the Wooster Group, an experimental theatre collective, which later on replaced the Performance Group. As Auslander argues, the Wooster Group is organised like experimental theatre collectives, but its role is different in that it questions 'the meaning, the very possibility of authenticity in postmodern culture' (Auslander, 1992: 84). In this sense it embodies the shift from a transgressive to a resistant approach to theatre.

This brief look at American political theatre serves two purposes. First of all, it shows the connotations and the function of political theatre in the United States, perceived as both agit-prop and theatre dealing with social and identity issues, including gay theatre, black theatre, chicano theatre, etc. When Peter Schumann was interviewed on *New York and Company*, a WNYC Radio programme, Leonard Leopate asked Schumann if political theatre is propaganda and if political theatre preaches to the converted and bores everyone else. Leopate's question confirms that in 1995, about sixty years after the FTP, political theatre was still perceived as being propaganda. Most important of all, political theatre has acquired a very fuzzy meaning in the United States, given that since the sixties everything can be political. Political has come to mean anything which is not highly commercial, which does not correspond to Broadway's standards and is not staged in mainstream theatres. The definition of political theatre functions as a handy label, a category to identify theatre texts that are disturbing, challenging and therefore difficult to stage. It is this use of the term that is particularly relevant to this analysis. Any play offering a provocative look at relevant issues affecting society can be dismissed as being political. Particularly in the United States, rather than identifying a theatrical genre, such a notion allows the categorisation, and in a number of cases, the refusal of a theatre which wants to stimulate social awareness, as well as entertain. As Ron Davis puts it:

> For most US theatres, commercial and not-for profit-alike, and for most US playgoers - and come to that, for most US critics - plays are produced for the so-called aesthetic satisfactions they can offer and tickets they can sell. Political in US jargon means a play about Democrats and Republicans. (1986: 318)

This aspect cannot be separated from a shift in American radical theatre which has inevitably affected its impact in political terms. The paradox of a left-wing theatre group like Belt and Braces creating a financially successful production similarly occurred in the United States. Davis's 1980-81 production of *We Won't Pay! We Won't Pay!* is an example of the transformation of a political play into a commercial show, despite his intention to maintain its political function. In this sense, the trajectory of Davis's theatrical career and the shift in his approach to political plays symbolises in many ways the evolution of American political theatre, which accounts for a generally depoliticised approach to Fo and Rame's work. It is therefore helpful to consider the role of Davis for a number of reasons, starting from the fact that he was the first director to introduce Fo's plays to the United States.[6]

Together with Davis, Ron Jenkins and Joel Schechter have largely contributed to the introduction of Fo's work in the United States. Schechter has supported the publication of Fo's texts as editor of the journal *Theater* and has been involved in the translation and staging of Fo's work on several occasions.[7] Jenkins has translated a number of Fo's plays, has written extensively on Fo's work and has been involved in Fo and Rame's American tours as stage interpreter, including most recently in 2000. But Davis's role in the presentation of Fo's plays in an American context contributed to the process of its commercialisation. For copyright reasons no other translation of *Non si paga! Non si paga!* could be made until 2001 when Jenkins published a new one, so Davis's version was the only text available for American productions. This is even more relevant if we consider that the American prèmiere of the play was staged by the San Francisco Mime Troupe. Davis, who had left the group, had already obtained the rights for his translation of the play, entitled *We Won't Pay! We Won't Pay!* As a consequence, the San Francisco Mime Troupe was only given amateur rights and their version was never staged again.

The San Francisco Mime Troupe production of *We Can't Pay? We Won't Pay!* was based on the combination of a British translation and an American translation, adapted by Joan Holden, the troupe's main playwright. Interestingly enough, the production was unusual for a number of reasons. It was not a play written by the troupe and it was performed indoors, rather than in one of the Bay Area parks, charging admission. They also toured the performance for a month in Southern California before bringing it to San Francisco, at the Victoria Theater, in December 1979. The San Francisco Mime Troupe decided to stage the play because they felt that Fo's style was similar to theirs. As explained by one of the actors, Lonnie Ford, 'We Can't Pay! We Won't Pay! couldn't have been more timely. America is just getting to the point where Italy has been since 1974' (quoted in Weiner, 1979). Moreover, according to the director Dan Chumley, 'though it deals with serious issues of survival, it is written in a style we – and our audiences – feel comfortable with: outrageous comedy, broad farcical conventions' (quoted in Weiner, 1979). In other words, the San Francisco Mime Troupe shared with Fo and Rame's 'La Comune' a commitment to political theatre as well as a collective structure, and they aimed at reproducing the political function of *We Can't Pay? We Won't Pay!* Most important of all, as Joan Holden argues:

---

[6] With the exception of a production of *Marcolfa* and *The Virtuous Burglar* in August 1969. The plays were translated and directed by Maurice Edwards at the Cubicolo, an off-Broadway theatre.

[7] Schechter was the dramaturge for the 1983 production of *About Face*, based on Dale McAdoo and Charles Mann's translation, staged at the Yale Repertory Theatre and directed by Andrei Belgrader. He also collaborated with Jenkins, Fo and Rame in revising Nelson's adaptation of *Accidental Death of an Anarchist* for the Broadway production.

The basic irony of Giovanni being a stalwart Communist would not make sense in America, I learned to leave the plays in Italy. The cultures and systems are so different that a great deal is lost if you transplant the stories to America. My approach as translator was to find American voices for the characters but to alter only those details that simply could not be understood here.[8]

As will be further shown, Holden's approach is the opposite of a common tendency to Americanise Fo's plays by inserting allusions to American politics, as in the case of the Broadway production of *Accidental Death of an Anarchist*. For all these reasons, the San Francisco Mime Troupe production was unusual and distinguished itself from following productions lacking a political challenge. The staging received mixed reviews. Among others, Bernard Weiner criticised the 'breaking of the fourth wall', i.e. the fact that the actors addressed the audience directly during the performance, but on the whole he defined the production as 'a rousing, fun show that provides much to think about' (Weiner, 1979).

By contrast, a more detailed glance at Davis's text shows to what extent it has influenced the American image of Fo's work. Davis has also been responsible for numerous productions of the play as a director, most of which will be analysed in this chapter. The following review of Davis's 1980-1981 production of *We Won't Pay! We Won't Pay!*, at the Chelsea Theater Centre, New York, points to the relevance of stage caricatures of Italians as the interpretative framework affecting Davis's approach. While acknowledging the limits of Davis's choice, Don Nelsen praises the director for succeeding in reinforcing those clichés:

Though there is room here for complaint about the stage Italian stereotype and segments that lag, 'Pay!' has found in R.G. Davis a translator and director who knows how to stage farce and who captures the flavor, the humour and the people of the Italian lower-class – at least as we know them from De Sica movies. (Nelsen, 1981)

The above comments indicate the stereotypical and above all theatrical nature of the image of Italians presented on the American stage. Davis had applied the same interpreting strategy used for his Vancouver staging of *We Won't Pay! We Won't Pay!* with a Canadian collective, the Tamanhous Theatre, in September 1980, as Christopher Dafoe's review shows:

The comedy is almost operatically played ... The characters are broadly drawn and the similarities of this production to a Marx Brothers film is, I suspect, no accident. Real Italians may complain that the characters on stage are *too* Italian to be real (if you know what I mean), but one understands fully why they are played this way. These are 'stage Italians' and the big emotions they display are entirely fitting in these circumstances. (Dafoe, 1980: 14)

---

[8] Telephone interview with Joan Holden, May 2004.

The writer underlines a predominant element of Davis's interpretative framework, i.e. the image of Italians conveyed by the Marx Brothers films, confirming the influence of cinema in reinforcing stereotypical notions of Italian culture. Furthermore, Dafoe acknowledges the caricaturing nature of 'stage Italians', but at the same time justifies their 'big emotions' and their exaggerated national traits because they represent a conventional stage rendition of Italians.

One of the main aspects of stage representations of Italians adopted by Davis was the use of the accent convention. Davis's claim about his use of Italian accents on the stage as a Brechtian 'distancing device' (Davis, 1986) contradicts the fact that he also used the accents, together with the gestures, as a tool to help American actors interpreting Italians on stage given the predominance of realistic acting training in the United States. As he emphasised when I interviewed him in 2000, the version of the Stanislavski system that has been adopted in America is the Method via Lee Strasberg and Harold Clurman of the Group Theatre. Davis argues that:

> The Method as developed in the United States, also called 'realistic acting' is a psychologically based form of developing emotional display that looks to be 'truthful' but is a lie, or looks to be 'honest' but is yet another distortion or naturalism. So one has a distortion of the Russian system, imported caviar with the lid off, and then used as if it were to display the 'truth'. The emphasis is psychologically simplistic displays of emotion.

When the guiding principle of the Stanislavski Method, as adopted in the United States, is applied to the performance of foreign plays, it means that actors need to display all those external traits, such as gesticulating and speaking with heavy accents, which make them appear 'authentic'.

But there is another aspect of the implications of the wide use of the Stanislavski Method that has affected American productions of Fo's plays. Davis claims that, since Fo's theatre comes from a different tradition, from the *commedia dell'arte*, from the Brechtian method, a play like *We Won't Pay! We Won't Pay!* is very hard to cast in the United States (Davis, 1981). This is also because actors with vaudeville experience, who would be more suited to interpret Fo's plays, do not want to take risks in doing political shows that can put their careers at risk. The difficulties in casting actors to perform Fo's plays in the United States because of their training is an aspect of the target theatrical system which, in Davis's opinion, has largely contributed to the American appropriation of Fo's plays, particularly in his 1980-1981 off-Broadway production of *We Won't Pay! We Won't Pay!* He claimed that in the last week of previews of the production its faults had become visible and he specifically related them to the acting style of actors performing in commercial theatre and their training. He identified such faults as follows: actors' inability to work together, misinterpretation of the characters, 'realistic styles intervening and the personalities of the actors changing the characters' (Davis,

1981: 35). He also emphasised how different this production was from his previous ones:

> In commercial terms it was a positive venture – anything with jokes that lasts more than three weeks off-Broadway is a success – but for me it was not enough. Without the heart of it – the lessons, the politics, the spirit, all those things one enjoyed in Vancouver and at NYU – the whole was but half.

In other words, Davis's staging of *We Won't Pay! We Won't Pay!* seemed to have followed a pattern similar to that of the Richards's staging of *Accidental Death of an Anarchist* in that they were both commercially successful – the New York show ran until 29 March 1981 for over one hundred performances. But to fully understand Davis's complaint about his own production one needs to take into account the history of the production and Davis's agenda, which show further aspects in common with Richards's strategy.

In the spring of 1980, while he was teaching at the New York University School of the Arts Theatre Programme, Davis presented a student production of the first act of *We Won't Pay! We Won't Pay!*, which was also staged at Town Hall as part of demonstration against the first United States denial of a visa to Fo and Rame. It was then that a producer invited him to stage the play off-Broadway. According to the *Village Voice* reviewer Charles Mann, Davis, as 'the *eminence grise* of the American independent radical theater' (1980: 114), was the ideal person to present Fo's work in the United States, despite the fact that he had left the San Francisco Mime Troupe in 1970. Similarly in the United Kingdom, Richards and Belt and Braces appeared to be the right interpreters of *Accidental Death of an Anarchist* given that they were important exponents of British political theatre. The similarities do not end here. Mann's comment that *We Won't Pay! We Won't Pay!* was Davis's 'first attempt to infiltrate the theatrical mainstream he spent half his career attacking' could similarly be applied to the staging of Richards's adaptation of *Accidental Death of an Anarchist* in the West End. Davis explained his intentions as follows:

> I've watched the political avant-garde drive itself into irrelevance. Now I want to get into American mainstream theater. ... I'm doing this play because I thought it might be commercial. I thought we could slip it right in a place like the Chelsea, message and all. ... It's easy to do, and it's got five actors and a million jokes, and the subject is right. ... Look at the front page of the *Times* and right in the first paragraph – Reagan's taking away all aid to cities with rent control, he's taking away CETA and welfare, and we're all about six inches away from being in the situation of the characters of the play. (ibid.)

There are different aspects of Davis's approach that need to be discussed for the purposes of this analysis. First, Davis's decision to stage Fo's play in an American mainstream theatre was a political choice. As he argues in his analysis of his productions of *We Won't Pay! We Won't Pay!*, published in *Theatre Quarterly*, his agenda as a theatre professional had changed since the 1960s:

In the 1960s my aim was to create work that could not be co-opted, and so we took a stance in alternative culture, rigidly antagonistic to the bourgeois variety. This position, too simplistic and no longer viable in the 1970s, required a review of the conditions and possibilities for the placement of left culture in the commercial markets. (Davis, 1981: 34)

Davis believed that alternative theatre as staged by a group like the San Francisco Mime Troupe was no longer effective. Rather than working in alternative circuits, Davis decided to infiltrate the theatrical establishment in New York. As he put it, his aim was 'to introduce a Marxist playwright into the American mainstream'.[9] Like postmodernist artists, he adopted a resistant approach rather than a transgressive one. Moreover, the social and political issues dealt with in the play appeared to be relevant to American society at the time, as emphasised by Davis. In his view, the play could potentially acquire a political function within the target society and therefore become an instrument to attack American bourgeois values by using commercial venues. In this sense there are significant commonalities between Davis and Richards's stagings of Fo's plays. While they both claimed the integrity of their political commitment, their productions contributed to the process of appropriation of Fo's work by the target culture, which, as previously shown, gave priority to the theatrical value of Fo's plays over their political challenge. This was due to the combination of a variety of factors, such as Davis and Richards's choices regarding the *mise en scène*, as well as the impact of the target theatrical systems, in terms of acting styles, theatrical traditions and audience expectations.

As Davis emphasised, Fo's play also had a series of advantages. *We Won't Pay! We Won't Pay!* is easy to produce, it has a relatively small cast and it is funny. The influence of extratextual factors, such as production costs and the number of actors required, in determining which foreign theatre texts get translated and how they are staged, is often underestimated, but, as in the case of this production, it is paramount. In Davis's view, *We Won't Pay! We Won't Pay!* had a further positive aspect. It was an Italian play and was set in Italy: 'People asked me, "Why choose some Italian play to do here?" "First, Brecht did that. He put a lot of his plays in foreign countries to get a little distance. You ain't in Italy, buddy, but your problems are"' (quoted in Mann, 1980).

Davis justified his choice once again for having that same distancing effect as the use of Italian accents on stage. What he is saying with this particular production is that staging foreign plays, dealing with social and political issues similar to those affecting American spectators, which do not represent a threat because set in another country, seems to be the only way to bring those issues to theatre. As emphasised in the previous chapter, the alterity of Fo's theatre in the British context played as much influence in that it contributed to its success,

---

[9] Telephone interview with Ron Davis, 2000.

particularly in the West End.[10] Davis's distancing approach functions in the same way as the strategy of detachment which, as Ron Jenkins claims, is the main aspect of American comedy. It was the trademark of Johnny Carson, one of the most successful American comedians. Referring to both Carson and Ronald Reagan, Jenkins explains: 'Instead of using laughter to defiantly mock injustice, they joked about the comic incongruities of our culture with a detachment that relieved them and their audience of any sense of responsibility for the social, political, and economic iniquities of their times.' (Jenkins, 1994: 205) Davis focused on creating the same sense of detachment in his productions of Fo's plays, by emphasising not only that they are set in a foreign land, but that they belong to a stereotypical Italy, to that image of Italy as a sunny Mediterranean country his spectators are so familiar with.

One clear example of Davis's approach to *We Won't Pay!* is the prologue that he has added in his translation of the play. It starts as follows:

> Buona serra, signor e signorini. I welcome you to NON SI PAGA, NON SI PAGA, WE WON'T PAY! WE WON'T PAY! My name is Fulvio Bardi. I am from the Italian tourist bureau and I have been asked by the producers of this show, because it is an Italian play, to speak to you about Italy and to encourage you to visit our beautiful country. (Fo, 1980: 15)

After referring to Ferraris, film stars such as Marcello Mastroianni and Sophia Loren, and encouraging the audience not to consider the play as being political, given that the characters are 'nice communists', the prologue continues:

> But if there should occur something in the play which you find too political, I suggest that you make use of an age-old Italian custom. Allow me to demonstrate: if you don't like what you hear, you put your hands like this (over ears). If you don't like what you see, you put your hands like this (over eyes). And if you don't like what you see and what you hear, you don't want to get involved, you raise your hands like this (Fuck-you gesture). (ibid.: 16)

Then the tourist issue is taken even further with the actor promoting Italian tours called 'The Mediterranean Sea: Cradle of Civilization and Home of the Fruit Fly' or 'Cardinal Cody Tour' free for women over seventy (ibid.: 17). Davis argues that he introduced the prologue 'to deflect the usual notions about political plays', as being too serious or heavy, and 'to explain something about the existence

---

[10] It is interesting to note that Fo made a similar statement about the setting of his plays. Robert Coe stated in his article that Fo had expanded his anti-American government satire because Italian audiences preferred to avoid dealing with national problems due to the atmosphere of repression in Italy. Fo argued: 'In Italy, you have to create some kind of distance and detour and talk about other, alien situations.' (quoted in Robert Coe, 1980: 43). One can argue that this was particularly the case at the end of the seventies in Italy since Italians were still shocked by the series of bombings and killings of those years.

of a Communist Party in Italy that was legitimate'.[11] Davis's assumption that his definition of Italian communists as 'conservative' in the prologue would provide American audiences with an understanding of the legitimate role of the Italian party is questionable. And it is interesting to note that in his 'production suggestions' preceding the translated text, Davis warns directors of the danger of separating the comedy from the politics in staging the play and reminds them of the importance of keeping a balance between the two. How they are supposed to do that when Davis's prologue suggests a reading of the play through an interpretative frame which calls for a caricaturing image of Italian culture, is difficult to understand. How can the audience engage with the provocative content of Fo's play when from the very beginning they are invited to imitate ridiculous gestures, supposedly Italian, and are offered cheap jokes like the following: 'This play is a work of art, and like all works of art, like Monet's *The Water Lilies*, for instance, it is a reflection of ... of ... water' (ibid.: 15). By inserting this classic farce gag Davis turns Fo's play into a comedy at the expense of its political value.

This is confirmed by Martin Gould's review:

> Fo's observations do have relevance to the situation of inflation in America but it simply does not seem as crucial here. This makes the audience only able to accept 'We Won't Pay' as a comedic entertainment and not as a political play. Fortunately, the play is more successful as a comedy; it offers some very amusing situations and characters. (Gould, 1980: 28)

Another journalist condemns Fo's work and praises Davis's direction for saving the production:

> Where 'We Won't Pay! We Won't Pay!' falls short is in its one dimensional message. Fo's indictments may well be taken, but they are repetitious and obvious. What actually saves the work from a one tone musical line is the spirited direction of R. G. Davis who manages to keep the action moving at breakneck speed. (Schaeffer, 1981: 20)

The author of the above review, together with other critics, ignores altogether Davis's interpretative and manipulative role as the translator and director of the foreign text. His intervention is only recognised as a compensation for the weak aspects of the play. The writer is clever in making a distinction between Davis's merit and Fo's faults and therefore attributing the 'repetitious and obvious indictments' to the Italian playwright, without considering that they might be so because of Davis's interpretation.

From September to October 1981 Davis directed yet another production of *We Won't Pay! We Won't Pay!* by the Los Angeles Actors Theatre (LAAT) with a cast of mainly black actors. As explained in the *LAAT Theatre Times*, black actors in the role of Italian working class families highlighted 'the similarities of the

---

[11] Telephone interview with Ron Davis, 2000.

elaborate social interplay that exists in the Italian and American Black working classes' (1981). In his programme notes, Davis summarised his two-and-a-half-year involvement with the play, including the evolution of the text and concluded as follows: 'We, of course, have turned and developed the text with the help of many actors who have read and performed it and the present company is part of that development.' The production received positive reviews. Polly Warfield praised Davis's direction and the casting and argued that 'It works wonderfully well to have the Italian working class couples portrayed by black actors' (1981). She continued by explaining that 'these working class strugglers are constantly confronted with the white man in multiple guise' (as police sergeant, undertaker, etc.), played by Joe Spano. In other words, the opposition between the working class and the institutional power was reinforced by the contrast between black and white people, adding an extra layer of significance relevant to American audiences.

In Ed Kaufman's opinion, the combination of comedy and politics of the play, of 'farce with Karl Marx's views', worked well in this 'classy' production (Kaufman, 1981). The critical response would seem to indicate that the production succeeded, at least to a certain extent, in reproducing the political function of the play. After New York, where Davis's strategy to challenge American theatrical establishment had failed, the Los Angeles production of *We Won't Pay! We Won't Pay!* was Davis's further attempt in staging this play with a political challenge. Interestingly enough, this became possible outside of New York, more precisely on the West Coast, an area where Fo and Rame's theatre was promoted by the San Francisco Mime Troupe, as well as the Eureka Theatre.[12]

In 1986 Davis published another article in *New Theatre Quarterly* about 'American approaches to Dario Fo', where he admits to his own responsibilities in relation to a mistaken representation of *Accidental Death of an Anarchist* in the United States: 'I will argue that all the North American productions of *Anarchist*, including my own, have failed to match the author's intentions, have misunderstood the structure of the work, and have not given enough importance to the casting of a recognisably political actor in the lead' (Davis, 1986: 313). Once again Davis emphasises the lack of political commitment of those who are involved in making Fo's work accessible to American audiences. He insists that the actor playing the role of the Fool in *Accidental Death of an Anarchist* needs to be 'a political person first and an actor second'. While it would certainly be ideal that Fo's interpreters shared his political views, we need to bear in mind that Fo is an actor, a man of theatre, as well as a 'political person', or better, that the two complement each other. Fo in fact is as interested in entertaining his audience as he

---

[12] In 1983 Davis also directed a production of the play in Spanish, with the title *No se paga! No se paga!*, at Teatro Cuarto in New York's Spanish Harlem. In Alice Salomon's view, Teatro Cuarto managed to challenge American spectators, 'to engage an audience in the play's issues and to send them home arguing over the different characters' contradicting ideological explanations of the play's events' (Salomon, 1983a: 64).

is in stimulating their thoughts, a point to which I will come back later. Last but not least, both the British and American history of Fo's theatre indicate that the political commitment of the interpreters of his work is only one element affecting the complex process of appropriation of his plays. Both Davis's and Richards's choices in adhering to the target cultural and theatrical systems when translating Fo's dramatic texts and directing their *mise en scène* have had a stronger effect than actors' lack of political commitment.

Another fundamental concern expressed by Davis testifies to another common aspect in the translation strategies adopted by British and American interpreters of Fo's work. As seen in the previous chapter, the same tendency to highlight the comic aspects of Fo's plays against the politics characterises the British appropriation of his work. The fact that Fo's plays can work as comedic rather than political entertainment is a fundamental aspect on which productions of his theatre in the United Kingdom and the United States rely. Given the close link between Fo's theatre and Italian political and social events, staging his plays as side-splitting farces aimed primarily at entertaining their audiences is a safer option. The 1984 Broadway production of *Accidental Death of an Anarchist* was criticised for presenting nothing else than superficial and banal references to the American political campaign of the time, instead of effectively challenging relevant social or political issues, as will be shown later.

A similar approach seems to have informed the 1983 production of *Tutta casa, letto e chiesa*. It was adapted, performed and directed by Estelle Parsons under the title of *Orgasmo Adulto Escapes from the Zoo* and staged at the Public Theater in New York. Because of the connotations that the notion of political theatre can assume in the United States, Parsons denied the political function of Rame's pieces altogether. In an interview with *The Village Voice*, Parsons argued that: 'To say that the plays are political is to minimize their depth. ... I was not interested in them from a message point of view. My attraction was really to their comic element and the challenge of the acting style that requires a relationship with the audience' (Salomon, 1983b). As Alisa Salomon comments, it is not surprising that Parsons denied the term 'political' because when it is applied to American theatre, it is considered synonymous of didacticism and dullness. By declaring that Rame's plays were not political, Parsons assured Central Park audiences that what they were going to see, or what they had seen, was not boring and didactic and that it did not challenge their own view of women's position in American society. She also believed that the only way to make the plays work in the United States would be by emphasising their Italianness. Interviewed by Jan Stuart, Parsons commented that the plays owed their success to their 'Milanese flavor' (Stuart, 1983). As previously argued, focusing on their foreign identity of playtexts allows target spectators to watch them without feeling threatened. It is interesting to note how Parson's approach to the play contradicts the fact that her performance was forbidden to young audiences. Anyone under 17 years of age was not admitted.

Despite the limits of the above-mentioned productions of Fo's plays, between the end of the 1970s and the beginning of the 1980s, his work started to be known in the United States, and American theatres and universities invited him to come to the United States and take part in festivals. The first time was in the spring of 1980 and this was also when he and Rame were refused a visa. Fo was supposed to perform *Mistero Buffo* during the Fifth Italian Theater Festival in New York City. The event was co-sponsored by New York University and the Italian Ministry of Arts but, as Fo argued a few years later:

> The Italian Foreign and Home Office intervened, urging the US government not to allow us in. And the American government had its own doubts whether it ought to let us have a visa. Why? Because we had for years been making satires about the United States, about the war in Vietnam, Chile, the ethnic minorities. (Fo, 1985b: 59)

The reason for the denial of a visa was reported in the press to be Fo and Rame's active involvement with *Soccorso Rosso*, an organisation which aimed at protecting the rights of left-wing political prisoners. More precisely, according to Section 212 (a) 28 of the Immigration Act 'aliens who write, publish, circulate, display or distribute any written or printed material advocating or teaching opposition to any organised government' are not allowed into the United States. This was at least the explanation given by unofficial spokesmen of the State Department, while the then United States Ambassador to Italy, Richard Gardner, refused to make any comment since, in his opinion, revealing the reasons for the denial of a visa would have reflected badly on Fo.[13] But Erika Munk in the *Village Voice* pointed to the contradictions of the government's attitude since a State Department spokesman acknowledged that Fo was accused not of terrorist activity, but simply of non-violent help to accused terrorists. Munk argued that it was absurd that the same procedure had been applied to other foreign writers in the past, making international dialogue subject to 'the idiot whim of State Department hacks'. To support her view, she reported the comment of Vittorio Brode, from the State Italian desk: 'Nobody in State thinks that Fo is going to foment revolution or throw bombs. It's just that Fo's record of performance with regard to the United States is not good' (Munk, 1980: 86).

In 1983 Fo and Rame were invited again to the United States, this time by Joseph Papp, the director of the Public Theater, to take part in the New York Shakespeare Festival. As explained by the State Department, they were forbidden to visit the United States a second time on similar grounds, again in relation to the McCarren-Walter Act which prevents those who support or are members of anarchist, Communist or terrorist organisations. This second denial of a visa to Fo and Rame provoked enormous protests by American intellectuals. Fo commented on the absurdity of the situation whereby he was banned from the country while his books were published and his plays put on stage (Fo, 1985: 59).

In 1984 Fo and Rame were also invited to a conference on the *Free Trade of Ideas* in Washington, but they were only able to take part in the discussion from

---

[13] See Mann 1980.

Toronto through a television connection.[14] Fo and Rame were finally granted permission to visit the United States only few weeks before the opening of the Broadway production of *Accidental Death of an Anarchist* in October 1984. During the press conference after their arrival in the United States, Fo emphasised that he had been denied a visa because of the pressures of the Italian government that wanted to prevent them from going to the United States. In particular he blamed the Home Affairs Minister and the Minister of Culture, Bernardo D'Arezzo, who had gone to the United States a few days before the decision to deny him a visa was taken and had managed to convince the American government. He then explained that the organisation 'Soccorso Rosso' was legal and that its funds and finances were publicly known. When asked why the Italian government might have tried to prevent his visit to the United States if Soccorso Rosso were a legal organisation, Fo emphasised the absurdity of such an attitude by telling the story of Eduardo De Filippo's funeral. Fo's speech was cut from the television broadcast of the funeral despite the fact the De Filippo family had asked him to talk and that the Italian president Pertini had approved his words. He also explained that if there were a real political reason for denying him and his wife a visa, in other words if the American government believed that they were connected to terrorist organisations, they would have not changed their minds.

The reason why Dario Fo was finally let into the country in 1984, as the producers of the Broadway show declared, was more commercial and business oriented than political or theatrical:

> Forget the free trade ideas. We appealed on the basis of free trade, period. ... We appealed as businessmen: my associates Alexander Cohen and Hildy Parks and I insisted on behalf of our backers, who were bankrolling 'Accidental Death' with a six-hundred-and-fifty-thousand capital investment ... We were claiming the same rights to pursue our business – unrestrained by unwarranted, arbitrary government's interference – that are enjoyed by international bankers, arms brokers, or any other buccaneers. (Anonymous, 1984: 40)

What the producers did was insist on the fact that they needed Fo to come and give his final advice on the show to ensure its success. If the author were not allowed in the country to give his opinion on the production, the government would be responsible for financial and artistic losses. In other words, the State Department let Fo and Rame enter the United States to avoid paying billions of dollars, which would have been the case if they had been sued by the producers. As Fo ironically commented, 'Portare in processo lo stato su una questione di affari in America è un fatto serio' (quoted in Provvedini, 1984: 31).[15] He also considered the budget of the

---

[14] The conference was sponsored by the American Civil Liberties Union and numerous other associations to examine the effects of the Reagan administration policy on intellectual and artistic exchanges.

[15] Taking the State to court for a business issue is a serious matter in America.

show to be excessive and he compared it to the modest figure of about fifty dollars (more or less 500 dollars in 1984) that he had spent to produce it in 1969-1970.

Although the financial issue was predominant, the decision was also partly influenced by the protests of American students, intellectuals and playwrights, who had opposed the government's decision from the beginning. In 1980 a show entitled 'An evening without Fo' was organised at the Town Hall, on Broadway. Arthur Miller and Martin Scorsese were present among others, and the New York University graduate acting students performed the first act of *We Won't Pay! We Won't Pay!* directed by Davis. Fo joked about the denial of the visa, saying that President Ronald Reagan was his agent and that he had called them and told them that he would deny them a visa a couple of times before allowing them into the country to give them a lot of publicity. He also added that Reagan's rival, Mondale, had lost the election because he wasn't as clever as Reagan in taking advantage of their story (Coppola, 1984: 34).

On a more serious note, Fo stated that another issue which contributed to convince the government was the fact that an electoral campaign was taking place and there had been a debate on television with several American intellectuals attacking the government for not allowing Fo into the United States. Mondale had often accused Reagan of denying human rights, during interviews and on television. So to sum up, Fo and Rame were finally granted a visa in 1984, mainly for financial reasons, after having been prevented from entering the country more than once for their alleged involvement with terrorist organisations, although it became clear that their political commitment was only a means for the government to justify the denial of a visa. Ironically, as Mel Gussow reported in *The New York Times*, in 1984 Fo was also given a work permit from the Immigration and Naturalization office, in which he was referred to as 'an alien of distinguished merit and ability' (Gussow, 1984b). But what makes the whole issue even more paradoxical is that though Fo was allowed to visit the United States to advise on the Broadway production of *Accidental Death of an Anarchist*, despite his presence the show was a total fiasco.

The American première of *Accidental Death of an Anarchist* ran from January to March 1983 at the Mark Taper Forum, Los Angeles, with the well-known film actor Ned Beatty in the leading role. It was adapted by John Lahr and directed by Mel Shapiro. Lahr's adaptation added references to Democrats, Republicans, and several American political events, with Fo's approval. But, in Davis's opinion, the adaptation combined with the director's approach, transformed the play into a 'banana-peel comedy' (Davis, 1986: 316). The Americanisation of the play on the whole did not succeed as confirmed by the negative critical reception. As will be shown, American adapters and directors' attempt at topicality, i.e. the strategy to contextualise political references, although encouraged by Fo, can make the play predictable and banal causing its failure in a number of cases, particularly the production at the Belasco Theatre, on Broadway.

In 1984 *Accidental Death of an Anarchist* was staged by the Arena Theatre Company, at the Kreeger Theater, in Washington DC, from 3 February to 18

March. It was adapted by the American playwright Richard Nelson (awarded the Obie Award in 1979 for his play *The Vienna Notes*) from a literal translation by Suzanne Cowan and directed by Douglas Wager. Nelson, like Lahr before him, had also had Fo's consent to fill up the text with American political references. More precisely, Jenkins and Schechter, in collaboration with Fo and Rame, were asked to adapt the text further to the political situation of the receiving society. The show was successful in Washington compared to the disaster on Broadway, where it was taken at the end of the same year and lasted only for two weeks.

According to Mitchell, despite the obstacles to the staging of Fo's work, previously emphasised, *Accidental Death of an Anarchist* made it to Broadway because the commercial success of Fo's plays in London encouraged American producers to stage his work in New York (Mitchell, 1999: 304).[16] When the production moved to New York, the leading role of the Fool was played by the British actor Jonathan Pryce, who was known for his Tony-winning acting in the 1976 play *Comedians* by Trevor Griffith. The show opened on 15 November and closed on Saturday 5 December, without any official announcement or comment in the press. Mel Gussow was already criticising the adaptation when it opened in Washington:

> The Arena version of the play is not as funny as the one anglicized and performed by Gavin Richards in London ... America would still seem to be in need of a true 'Anarchist' adaptation. On the other hand the director and adapter have effectively played up the theatrical side of the comedy. (Gussow, 1984a)

The claim that the political allusions inserted in the adaptation were too obvious and superficial was one of the main issues that caused the failure of the show at the Belasco Theatre. The reviewer here makes a distinction between the political aspect of Fo's play and the 'theatrical side', confirming once more the tendency in American stagings of Fo's work to highlight the second. For example, the show started with a huge mock-up front page of an Italian newspaper in the background, with the news of 'the accidental death of an anarchist'. From the very beginning the leading actor interacted with the audience by reading the first lines of the article, then translating it for the audience, while mocking the author who was seen in a large photograph. Moreover during the show, he often pretended to be confused by saying: 'The United States ... pardon, Italy', thus emphasising the parallel between the two countries.

The main contradictions emphasised in relation to British stagings of Fo's plays similarly characterise American productions. Critics' comments like the following about the nature of Americanised Fo echoed those of British reviewers who

---

[16] Similarly Zeffirelli's productions of De Filippo's *Saturday, Sunday, Monday* and *Filumena* were brought to New York with the hope that the London success could be duplicated in the United States.

lamented the transformation of Fo into a trendy bourgeois playwright as a result of the British appropriation of his theatre:

> Nelson's adaptation curiously attempts to Americanize the play's dialogue without altering its Roman setting and Roman characters. The result is a hodgepodge, farcical rather than satirical; whatever Swiftian indignation may have lacerated Fo's breast in Italian, in English he emerges as a sort of literary marshmallow, tasteless on principle and gooey at the core. (Gill, 1984: 182)

But while Richards's production of *Accidental Death of an Anarchist* was very successful, the Broadway staging failed mainly because of Frank Rich's negative review that appeared in *The New York Times* on 16 November 1984, as Fo argues.[17] After his article was published, a number of negative reviews appeared in other newspapers like *The Village Voice* and *The Christian Science Monitor*, among others. Frank Rich condemned the production in the opening lines of his article:

> Until the State Department at last lifted its ban and granted him a visa this month, the leftist Italian playwright Dario Fo was deemed too incendiary to be admitted into the United States. Theatergoers who now visit the first Broadway production of a Fo work, *Accidental Death of an Anarchist* can't be blamed if they wonder what all the fuss was about. The farce at Belasco is considerably less biting than the average David Letterman monologue and not nearly as funny. (Rich, 1984: 3)

Half way down the page, the writer referred to the possibility that the shortcomings of the play might not be entirely Fo's fault: 'It's possible that not all of these comic inventions are Mr Fo's own – and that his native, populist theatrical style had been sanitized for New York consumption.' But readers and audiences were left to decide to what extent the Broadway show represented Fo's play. The risk was that American theatres could decide not to stage his plays again and that the Broadway fiasco might discourage an interest in the Italian playwright, as Mel Gussow feared (1984c).

Erika Munk in the *Village Voice* attacked the show as fiercely as Frank Rich. She condemned the production for being 'a travesty' as the result of the director's interpreting strategy in making the play entertaining at all costs. 'Mafia tics', as she defined them, were some of the caricaturing elements of the show and Joe Grifasi impersonated the stereotype of a dumb Italian police captain (Munk, 1984). In an interview with Alisa Salomon, Fo criticised Wager's directorial choices for undermining the anger of the policemen and replacing it with clowning (Salomon, 1984). Given the fundamental interrelation between the ideology informing his plays and their comic nature, adapting his plays to the current political situation of the target culture is only one aspect of the translation of his work. If the *mise en*

---

[17] Telephone interview with Dario Fo, Febuary 2000.

scène of *Accidental Death* is informed by the 'stage immigrant' meta-text, by portraying the policemen as stereotypical Italian figures, the whole aspect of the brutality and corruption of the police force is cut off, altering the overall coherence of the text, as occurred in Richards's production of the play. Fo reiterated this, pointing also to the anachronistic nature of such clichés:

> L'anarchico nella versione di Broadway aveva un difetto di fondo: era troppo edulcorato. Gli attori erano bravi, ma mancava la cattiveria e la tragedia. C'era questa preoccupazione insopportabile di fare la caricatura dell'italiano visto ancora in chiave anacronistica: un personaggio con baffi e basette più adatto a fare la pubblicità degli spaghetti al pomodoro. (quoted in Fontanella, 1987: 28)[18]

As previously indicated, a tendency to caricature and play down the tragic aspects of the social conditions represented in Fo's work is not limited to the Broadway show. It appears over and over again in foreign productions of his plays, and in particular in the English-speaking world. Fo states that the grotesque, the comic aspect of his work is as relevant as the political content, that first and foremost his plays need to work as theatre texts, need to entertain his audience before challenging them. This is why *Accidental Death of an Anarchist*, considered the perfect example of political theatre, can be successful even when its political nature has been downplayed:

> Questo gioco del grottesco, del paradosso, della follia è un gioco che potrebbe benissimo stare in piedi anche senza il discorso politico. Tant'è vero che alcuni registi (Dio li castighi a macchina), preoccupati di realizzare un puro divertimento, hanno tolto di mezzo l'indicazione realistica del conflitto, hanno esasperato il gioco comico fino a renderlo clownesco e alla fine hanno ottenuto una specie di *pochade* surreale dove ci si sganascia, uscendo poi di teatro ben svuotati di ogni indignazione o pensiero molesto. È questa l'operazione che hanno condotto a New York, al Belasco dove tutto il discorso politico era stato letteralmente assassinato. Ma la macchina teatrale stava in piedi lo stesso. (Fo, 1990a: 149)[19]

---

[18] 'The Anarchist in the Broadway version had a fundamental fault: the play had been sugarcoated too much. The actors were good, but the viciousness and tragedy were missing. There was this unbearable concern to make a caricature of the Italians according to an anachronistic perspective: a character with moustache and side whiskers more appropriate to advertising spaghetti with tomato sauce.'

[19] 'The aspect of grotesque, of paradox, of madness is a kind of game which might work perfectly even without political commitment. This is confirmed by the fact that some directors, focusing mainly on creating a play of pure entertainment, have taken away the realistic connotation of the conflict, have exaggerated the comical game to the point of making it clownish and in the end they have come up with a sort of surreal pochade which makes everybody laugh his head off and leave the theatre without any sense of indignation or any disturbing thought. This is the strategy which was adopted in New York, at the Belasco Theatre where all the political discourse was literally murdered. But despite it all the theatrical machine worked.'

The fundamentally comic aspect of Fo's work, combined with the supposed hostility towards political theatre in the United States, can be used as a justification by directors and adapters of Fo's plays to manipulate them.

When Matthew Fleury in an interview with Fo, told him that European political plays do not work in the United States because they are not relevant to most Americans, Fo replied as follows:

> Sometimes the reason for such failure originates in the strange mania on the part of American writers for meddling with the texts of European writers. The producer and director of the Washington production at first inserted songs and altered the text. It was a disaster. ... They had this idea that everything should be simplified for the American mind. This is an insult to the American people. (Fleury, 1985: 76)

Not only is there this tendency to simplify foreign plays to make them accessible to American audiences, but emphasising the foreignness of Italian politics becomes also a way of denying the relevance of certain social and political issues that do have parallels in American culture. For example, the brutality and corruption of the police force characterising the case of the anarchist Pinelli emerges from a number of American events, such as the death of the anarchist Andrea Salsedo who fell from the 14th floor of the New York Police Department on 3 May 1920 after having been held for eight weeks illegally, and the case of the anarchists Sacco and Vanzetti whose execution in 1927 generated a worldwide debate because they were believed to be innocent. Despite the fact that these notorious cases go back to the 1920s, events of police brutality in the United States were not at all a thing of the past in 1984 and are not so in recent years, since in February 1999 a black unarmed African immigrant was brutally killed by the New York police and the policemen were not found guilty.

Some critics used this production of *Accidental Death of an Anarchist* as an example to prove that Fo's theatre cannot be staged successfully in the United States because the Italian theatrical heritage is too different from the American. Howard Kissel, for example, argued that:

> The device of having a clown interact with caricatured 'real people', one suspects, might be a commonplace in Italy, where one can find traces of commedia dell'arte even in films. Here there is no real counterpart. For us a character changing costumes, slipping in and out of personae and making wisecracks, sometimes in the style of Groucho Marx, seems closer to cabaret than theater ... mainly it is an evening of verbal and visual gags and some topical references to the recent election (which are probably the contribution of the American playwright Richard Nelson, who 'adapted' Fo's script). (Kissel, 1984)

The responsibilities of the adapter here are only tentatively acknowledged in brackets. Kissel treated the American *mise en scène* as an exact reproduction of the source text and argued that now that American audiences could look at this play 'more directly' it was clear that Fo's theatre was nothing more than cabaret. What is even more interesting is the meta-text that the author of the article brings to this particular *mise en scène*. He started from the assumption that the style and techniques of *commedia dell'arte* affect not only Italian theatre, but even Italian cinema. Such a misleading assumption allows the journalist to overemphasise the differences between Italian and American theatre traditions in order to support his view of the uniqueness of Fo's theatre and the subsequent difficulties in integrating it into the target cultural context.

If the isolationism of American theatre, the connotation of political theatre in the United States, the differences in actor training and theatre traditions are among the most relevant aspects affecting American *mises en scène* of Italian plays, in the case of *Accidental Death*'s failure on Broadway, the influence of the press response outweighed all other factors. This is borne out by the fact that before 1984, other productions had been staged, both in the United Kingdom and in the United States, reflecting the same kind of approach negating Fo's ideology, but which were nevertheless successful, like Davis's staging of *We Won't Pay! We Won't Pay!* and the London staging of *Accidental Death*. David Kaufman made an interesting comment on the expectations that the denial of a visa to Fo and Rame had created, and wondered if the production could have met such high expectations given that it was the result of 'a veritable scandal of intercultural affairs'. In his opinion, after such an incredible build up, after being defined as the most incendiary work of a political playwright, the response to the opening of the show was inevitably anticlimactic. Above all, he argued: 'It demonstrated the covert power of the media, and the culture which it ostensibly serves to co-opt anything valid with over-attention' (Kaufman, 1984).

The expectations created by the denial of a visa to Fo and Rame and the subsequent perception of their work as so provocative as to represent a threat to American society, had indeed a paramount influence. As previously indicated, spectators bring to theatre a horizon of expectations which is inevitably affected by each production they see.[20] This is particularly true in the case of the 1984 American production of *Accidental Death of an Anarchist*. As Susan Bennett argues:

> In North America, the depoliticizing at the production stage destroyed the play. As *Anarchist* is structured politically and relies on involving the political sense of audiences, it is hardly surprising that North American audiences were merely confused. Any expectations of a Marxist play were thwarted and thus the pleasure of endorsement, speculation, or rejection denied. (Bennett, 1990: 108)

But the disappointment caused by the fact that Fo's theatre, as staged on

---

[20] As Susan Bennett argues, 'The spectator comes to the theatre as a member of an already-constituted interpretative community and also brings a horizon of expectations shaped by the pre-performance elements. ... That horizon of expectations is never fixed and is always tested by, among other things, the range of theatre available, the play, and the particular production' (Bennett, 1990: 149).

Broadway, appeared to be anything but provocative and revolutionary, seems to have particularly affected the response of the critics. We can only speculate on how successful the show might have been if Frank Rich had written a different review, or if the producers had decided to let the show run a little longer. But what was the audience's reaction to the production?

While there was hardly any mention of spectators' response in the American press, Italian reviewers reported that the show was sold out during the previews – when the tickets were at reduced price – and the public enjoyed it. Several Italian reviewers who went to the previews emphasised the show's success and its audience's enjoyment. Stefano Trincia described the spectators' attitude as very positive throughout the show: 'risate scroscianti durante tutto l'arco dello spettacolo, alla fine quasi un'ovazione' (Trincia, 1984).[21] Luciana Capretti, journalist for *Il Giorno*, wrote that the show was received by the audience with great enthusiasm (Capretti, 1984). This confirms two issues involved in the reception of this play. First, despite the reservations that Fo and critics alike had about the Broadway *mise en scène*, the audience seemed to like it. Second, it testifies to the 'covert power of the media' since what was considered the failure of the show seems to have been caused mainly by the negative review in a major American newspaper, which contrasts with the audience's reaction, as testified to by Italian reporters.

Having said that, it is important to bear in mind that behind the apparent uniformity of public reaction, individual responses are equally significant. While there are common aspects shared by the majority of spectators in their relation to a particular play, audiences are nevertheless constituted by individuals who inevitably react differently according to their personal experiences and tastes. As Bennett puts it, 'While audience homogeneity would seem to be most likely, it is worth remembering the vulnerability of that united response.' (Bennett, 1990: 164) Edwin Wilson in the *Wall Street Journal* emphasised the appreciation of the show by a specific group among the audience, city professionals, as proof that the political nature of the show had been downplayed. The American version of the play included a series of phrases taken from Reagan and Bush campaign speeches, such as 'this is the greatest country on earth', 'there is a job for everyone' and 'This is a land rich in resources, and the richest resource of all is our rich people.' In Wilson's view, the fact that a group of bankers and lawyers told him that they enjoyed the play, 'especially the line about our richest resource being the rich', indicated how 'sugarcoated' were the politics of the play since they didn't feel threatened by the play's anti-capitalist satire. (Wilson, 1984) Within the largest group of the audience as a whole, this particular sub-group of spectators shared the general appreciation of the show, but through an interpretative process which contrasts with 'received' readings of the play.[22]

---

[21] 'Roaring laugther during the whole performance, at the end almost a standing ovation.'

[22] In Bennett's view, 'It is not an easy task to locate a set pattern of responses even for theatre which represents a recognizable cultural product, the play produced by mainstream

The whole issue of the contrast between the audience's reaction and the critics' approach is as relevant, in my view, as the translation strategy adopted by Richard Nelson in transposing the text into American English. The relationship with the public is, in fact, a major element of Fo and Rame's theatre, as Fo argues:

> A me piace recitare, e per farlo bisogna avere un pubblico, un muro non sarebbe la stessa cosa. E se a uno non piace, se non gode nell'effervescenza che il pubblico determina, in quella specie di coinvolgimento l'un l'altro determinato dal rapporto della risata, è inutile che pensi a fare il commediante. Le reazioni del pubblico sono corrispondenze, addirittura giochi di appoggio, sostegno che dà a quello che fai. La gente ti suggerisce i ritmi, i tempi, le assonanze, fa capire che devi tagliare una battuta o che è inutile insistere su una chiave che ormai è risolta con una situazione. Il pubblico è la mia cartina di tornasole, in ogni momento. (quoted in Dall'Osso, 1984: 31)[23]

During their 1986 tour in the United States, Fo and Rame's relationship with American audiences was their main focus. Their tour was extremely successful: every night their show was sold out and praised by critics, actors and playwrights. They were continually invited to perform all over the United States. Among other things, they were also invited to the Obies night, the Oscar for the off-off-Broadway and performed in front of theatre experts, directors and actors.

In an interview with Claudio Gatti, Fo explained that he and Rame had decided to go to the United States, among other reasons, because there were several American theatre companies staging altered and distorted versions of their plays. Therefore, they wanted to show Americans how they performed their own shows, as well as to know more about American theatre (Gatti, 1986: 48). Rame expressed the same view on American adaptations of their shows: 'Era importante mostrare finalmente agli americani com'è il nostro teatro fatto da noi. Perché loro riducono tutto in farsa.' (Capretti, 1986: 52)[24] Before performing for an American public, Fo had been warned by intellectuals about the difficulties of presenting his theatre to American audiences, but instead he succeeded in creating a stimulating relationship with American theatre-goers.[25] The first shows were in Boston for an

---

organizations.' (1990: 103). The task is even more difficult in relation to non mainstream plays, such as *Accidental Death*, subject to the manipulative process involved in translation.

[23] 'I like performing, and to do that you need an audience, a wall would not be the same. And if one doesn't like that, if one doesn't enjoy the excitement provoked by the audience, in that reciprocal involvement determined by laughter, there is no point in being a comedian. Audience's reactions are correspondences, even games of support, support for what you do. People suggest to you the rhythms, the timing, the assonances, they make you understand when you need to cut a line or that it is pointless to insist on what has already been solved with a situation. The audience is a litmus test, for every moment.'

[24] 'It was important to show American people what our theatre is like done by us. Because they reduce everything to farce.'

[25] Fo commented as follows: 'Gli intellettuali ci avevano detto di stare attenti: che ne sanno gli americani del medioevo? Come possono riderne? Il nostro teatro, il nostro umorismo,

audience mainly made up of students and intellectuals. Fo had also been warned about the unusual composition of his Boston public, but he proved successful in relating to people from a number of American cities. He also explained that the audience laughed at his jokes on Reagan and on American politics and elaborated further, 'forse perché il reaganismo sta uccidendo una tradizione di satira politica che era estremamente radicata' (ibid.).[26] He justified his success as the result of American audiences' need for political satire. For example, American spectators laughed at his imitations of Reagan's mistakes, such as when he talked about poor people. Fo argued that his rapport with the public was the best aspect of his tour and made an interesting observation on Americans' reaction to his shows: 'Penso che il pubblico abbia capito, soprattutto che si può fare un pezzo serio senza l'urlo, il patetico, la demagogia. Insomma, senza il melodramma' (Gatti, 1986: 51).[27] Fo and Rame provided American spectators with a different image of their work and showed an alternative to the naturalistic approach so often adopted in productions of Italian theatre.

One main difference, remarked on by Fo, between the critics' response to his theatre in Italy and in the United States, was that while American reviewers praised his work, his technique, his humour and satire, they did not mention his ideology at all. Audiences, instead, wanted to talk about politics. People arrived at the show prepared, they talked among themselves, they brought friends, as Fo claimed (1986: 30). Again a contrast between audience and critics emerges in the American approach to Fo's work. Despite their enthusiasm, though, American audiences were prepared to take on Fo's provocation only to a certain extent. There were a number of topics which were taboo, like sexuality and eroticism, together with social status, wealth and national pride. During his performance of *Mistero Buffo* in 1986, Fo told a joke about the Italian flag and how he had found a restaurant in Belgium where the table cloth had the Italian flag on. When he said he could do the same with the American flag, there was a dead silence.

Franca Rame's show, *Tutto casa, letto e chiesa,*[28] was almost as successful as *Mistero Buffo* and she was enthusiastic about American women's reaction: 'Sembra di essere a Milano, con tutti quegli applausi e quelle urla. Dopo il brano sullo stupro e la violenza c'erano donne che venivano ad abbracciarmi, a regalarmi

---

dicevano tutti, sono profondamente europei. E invece, le due serate sono state un successo incredibile, sorprendente, sia per Franca che per me' [Intellectuals had told us to be careful: what do Americans know about the Middle Ages? How can they laugh? Our theatre, our humour, they all said, are deeply European. But, instead, both nights were an incredible success, surprising both for Franca and myself] (Quoted in Miretti, 1986: 27).

[26] 'Perhaps because Reaganism is killing a tradition of political satire which was well rooted.'

[27] 'I think that the audience understood, above all that you can do a piece without making it loud, or being pathetic, without demagogy. In other words, without melodrama.'

[28] She performed four more monologues from *Tutto casa, letto e chiesa*: *Il risveglio*, *Abbiamo tutte la stessa storia*, *Medea* and *Una donna sola*.

un fiore, alcune tra le lacrime' (Farkas, 1986:35).[29] Despite Rame's comments quoted above, the response of American female spectators and critics was not always so positive. Although journalists recognised her abilities as an actress, they were much more critical about the validity of her feminist message. Mel Gussow commented that while her passion was genuine and admirable, what she said about women's sexual and political slavery appeared rather simplistic from an American perspective (Gussow, 1986). According to Maria Nadotti, American spectators either liked her a lot or were annoyed by her. Some militant feminists attacked her and patronised her, judging her analysis of women's condition in society out of date (Nadotti, 1986). The American press kept on comparing the two actors and insisting that Fo was a better actor than Rame. This praise of Fo's abilities over Rame's acting has often emerged in the Italian press, as Rame emphasises:

> Oggi Dario è intoccabile e anche il critico più astioso e prevenuto non si giocherebbe la propria credibilità ... Possono fare altro i nostri detrattori. L'hanno fatto. Lo fanno. 'Certo con Dario in scena gli spettacoli sono ben altra cosa!' Il teatro di Fo non si discute. Ma Franca Rame! 'La suffragetta! La passionaria' ... Hanno cercato di dividerci sulla diversità dei due 'teatri'. ... Non ci sono due teatri, uno di Dario e uno di Franca. C'è il nostro teatro. (Della Mea, 1986: 43)[30]

Nadotti believes that this was mainly due to the fact that Rame talks about issues such as sex and sexual violence, which are taboo in a puritan country like the United States. Her opinion is confirmed by the fact that the indecent language and obscenities of Fo's show instead were never criticised. A number of critics argued that the women portrayed in Rame's shows, victims of men and their violence, do not exist any more, or maybe exist only in Italy and certainly not in such a developed society as America. This was also Howard Kissel's opinion when *Orgasmo Adulto Escapes from the Zoo* was performed by Estelle Parsons during the 1983 New York Shakespeare Festival:

> Although the plays cover a variety of times and places their overall mood is simplistic and heavyhanded. Some of these plays were evidently first performed by Rame for the peasants of Tuscany and she may have indeed raised the consciousness of those victims of centuries of male oppression, who may have never noticed before that they have been mistreated. ... but they present ironies that will not be considered revelations to the

---

[29] 'It was like being in Milan, with all those applauses and people screaming. After the piece on rape and violence, women came to hug me, some gave me flowers, some of them were in tears.'
[30] 'Nowadays Dario cannot be criticised and even the most bitter and prejudiced critic would not put his credibility at risk. Our denigrators can do better. They have done better. They do better. 'With Dario on stage performances are a different matter altogether.' Fo's theatre is beyond criticism. But Franca Rame! 'The suffragette! The passionate one' ... They have tried to divide us on the basis of the diversity of the two 'theatres' ... there is no such a thing as two theatres, one by Dario and one by Franca. There is our theatre.'

Central Park West and West End Avenue liberals who constitute the logical audience for this work. (Kissel, 1984:18)

Such an attitude is the result of a dismissive approach, that is little more than a disturbing comment on one's own culture. As Nadotti argues, 'È vero che dà fastidio che venga qualcuno a dirti che il re è nudo, soprattutto se non ti dice poi che c'è modo di rivestirlo' (Nadotti, 1986: 63).[31]

One can argue that the more critical response to Rame's work is related to the fact that Rame's plays are characterised by a more serious and disturbing tone. Some of her portraits of women are funny and satirical, but others like *Stupro*, based on Rame's rape, are disconcerting, they touch the audience on a much deeper emotional level. *Stupro*, in particular, reminds Americans of the thousands of rapes perpetrated in the United States, despite the fact that many try to pretend that they do not take place. It is much more convenient and self reassuring to say that American women are now emancipated and that those issues are relevant only in a backward country like Italy.

At this point it will be useful to look at productions representing an exception to the Americanising approach analysed so far in their attempt to reproduce the political function of Fo and Rame's plays, like those based on Jenkins's translations and those staged by a San Francisco leading theatre group, the Eureka Theatre Company (one of which was also a translation by Jenkins). For the purposes of the present analysis it is more useful to begin with Jenkins's translations even though they chronologically come after the Eureka Theatre stagings. They are the 1987 American première of *Archangels Don't Play Pinball* (*Gli arcangeli non giocano al flipper*) staged by the American Repertory Theatre, Cambridge and the 1989 staging of *The Story of the Tiger* (*La storia della tigre*) at the Charlestown Working Theatre, Boston. Both of them are the result of a close collaboration between Jenkins, Fo and Rame, in terms of dramatic text and *mise en scène*. In particular, *Archangels Don't Play Pinball* was also directed by Fo and Rame. It is important to bear in mind that the play was written in 1959, which means that it belongs to Fo and Rame's 'bourgeois period', when they staged a number of plays at the Teatro Odeon. It is the story of a group of petty criminals, 'balordi', set in the outskirts of Milan. The protagonist is tricked by his friends into marrying a prostitute, and the fact that he tries to find a new identity triggers a whole series of farcical situations. As Mitchell points out, the play satirises the government burocracy and ministers' corruption within a Brechtian frame (Mitchell, 1999).

What is interesting is that, despite Fo and Rame's direction, the ART production was criticised for trying too hard to be topical. Julian West wrote: 'It seems that Fo cut the headlines out of the papers over the last weeks and pasted them into the script. A blow for topicality ... but not for humour' (West, 1987).

---

[31] 'It is true that it bothers us if somebody tells that the king is naked, above all if he does not say that there is a way to get him dressed again.'

Needless to say, the above criticisms sound very much like those addressed to productions of *Accidental Death of an Anarchist*. The history of American Fo seemed to repeat itself, also in terms of audience and critics' expectations towards Fo's theatre. It was hoped that the première of *Archangels Don't Play Pinball*, concluding a difficult year for the ART for a number of risky stagings under Robert Brustein's artistic direction, would have redeemed the season. But, as Dann Kosow put it: 'Unfortunately, the anticipation proved more exciting than the realization.' (Kosow, 1987) Carolyn Clay clearly explained the reasons for such a strong disappointment as follows:

> Its failure is as disappointing as it is baffling – disappointing because expectations were high, baffling because – with four directors (the Fos, associate director Arturo Corso, and assistant director Ron Jenkins) in addition to Brustein on hand – someone should surely have caught on that things weren't making it over cultural and linguistic barriers. (Clay, 1987)

While Fo gave some advice for the Broadway production of *Accidental Death of an Anarchist*, here he played a multiple role, since he designed the set and costumes, as well as co-directing the play. But much of the humour was considered to have been misplaced, from superficial political jabs at Ronald Reagan down to the choice of the protagonist's name, 'Il Lungo' in Italian, as Sunny Cloudy Stormy Weather, played by Geoff Hoyle. The latter, known for having performed in other Fo's plays on the West Coast, was praised for his performance.

Fo opened the show with a pre-curtain speech in which he explained that the play had been updated and, among other things, made jokes about Ronald Reagan, such as the following: 'Who would have thought Ronald Reagan would still be an actor.' Fo's opening was considered by many as the hightlight of the performance. Frank Dolan's comments are revealing in this sense:

> The truth is the production is an embarassment for the Fos and the actors. It is unfunny to a terrible degree. When Dario gave a pre-curtain speech he was hilarious and had the audience in the palm of his hand. When the curtain opened everything died. It is a sad commentary on the fact that this 'Italian tradition' does not work well 'americanized'. (Dolan, 1987)

Fo's mini performance in Italian, translated on stage by Jenkins, was much more appreciated than the entire show, which was in English. On the contrary, Fo and Rame's direction and updating of the play was far from being a guarantee for the production's political effectiveness. According to Richard Seyd, the problem was that 'Fo tried to impose Italian theatrical rhythms to the English language.'[32] This production of *Archangels Don't Play Pinball* also confirms Dolan's view that Fo and Rame's plays do not work when they are Americanised if as a result there is a clash between the contextualised political content and the original comedy.

---

[32] Telephone interview, June 2004.

In 1989 Tommy Derrah performed Jenkins's translation of *The Story of the Tiger*, staged as part of a double bill entitled *Fo's Fables* together with *The Diary of Eve*, at the Charlestown Working Theater. The latter is a community theatre and this is its mission statement: 'We offer to our participants and audiences new visions and understandings of the world around us by combining professional artistry with community spirit. The Charlestown Working Theater seeks to entertain, inform and inspire.'[33] The monologue was staged with a Chinese text and the image of a tiger in the background. Derrah and Jenkins added a prologue, consulting with Fo, explaining the origins of the play based on a story that Fo had heard from a Shanghai storyteller. This is an ancient legend about a wounded Communist soldier who is found and nursed by a tigress. Fo rewrote the story in dialect emphasising its political significance since the tiger symbolises man's spirit of self-determination, particularly applied to the working-class struggle. Similarly, the prologue in English focuses above all on the play's political function, informing the audience that in 1988 Fo updated and performed *The Story of the Tiger* for a demonstration in Milan supporting the cause of the Chinese students of Tianamen Square.

The American production aimed at maintaining such political commitment, and Derrah concluded the prologue as follows: 'Every time I imagine the tiger roaring in Dario's play, I hear the voices of the demonstrators in Tianamen Square, and I'd like to dedicate the play to them, with the hope that those voices will be remembered long after they've disappeared from the evening news' (Jenkins, 1990: 40). The nature of the play, particularly the fact that it is a one-man show, allowed Jenkins and Derrah to present a different Fo to American audiences. As will also be shown in the next chapter, a one-man show, relying on the acting style of only one actor, encourages by definition the challenge to dominant American theatre practices more than other plays requiring a larger cast. Among others, Chris Ertel praised Derrah's 'tremendous versatility and control' (1989), and Arthur Friedman argued that 'Derrah's performance is a technical tour-de-force of such humour and variety it justifies the entire double bill' (1989).

Having said that, the Eureka Theatre Company successfully staged a number of plays, including *Accidental Death of an Anarchist*[34] and *About Face (Claxon, trombette e pernacchie)*.[35] More precisely, the Eureka Theatre production of *Accidental Death of an Anarchist*, in which the well-known clown Geoff Hoyle played the Fool, was a huge success. Such a contrast between this production and the one on Broadway, which opened a week later, tells us a great deal about the impact that translation strategies have had on stagings of Fo and Rame's plays. Holden in fact chose not to Americanise the play. In Holden's view, the success of

---

[33] See www.charlestownworkingtheater.org.

[34] Translated and adapted by Joan Holden and directed by Anthony Taccone in 1984.

[35] Translated by Ron Jenkins and directed by Richard Seyd, it was first staged in San Francisco in 1985 and then in 1987 in a joint revival with the Metropolitan Theater, at the TOMI Theater in New York.

Accidental Death of an Anarchist, together with the previous San Francisco Mime Troupe production of *We Can't Pay! We Won't Pay!*, confirmed that audiences validated their choice not to localise Fo's plays.[36] Dan Sullivan, among others, argued that, whereas the play didn't work on Broadway, 'Finally an American company has got Dario Fo's Accidental Death of an Anarchist right. ... Finally we see how "Accidental Death" was able to run for months in London. Not just because it's a pointed play, but because it's truly a funny one' (Sullivan, 1984). Moreover, he explained how effective was Holden's choice to keep the 1970s Italian setting by arguing that 'We are put on the alert to look for the very parallels that the production seems to be denying. In this way the production doesn't have to translate the action to America – we're doing so in our own heads' (ibid.). Bernard Weiner similarly argued that the Eureka production was 'a strong, often hilarious treatment of this engaging political farce' (Weiner, 1984). Weiner rightly pointed to what is a vital factor for a successful staging of this play: 'an ensemble well trained in physical comedy and a wild comic style'. The Eureka production in fact boasted an excellent cast which included two former actors of the San Francisco Mime Troupe, Joe Bellan and Andrew Snow, together with Hoyle. Holden's translating approach combined with a well trained cast proves that *Accidental Death of an Anarchist* can be successfully staged without losing its unique mixture of comedy and political commitment.

The same can be said for the 1985 Eureka production of *About Face*, which was not transposed to an American context. Despite the problems of translating and staging this play for non-Italian audiences, analysed in the previous chapter, the Eureka theatre production was successful. It was defined as 'a superb production' and 'the funniest, most enjoyable show in town' (Esta, 1985). The cast, as in the case of *Accidental Death of an Anarchist*, included former San Francisco Mime Troupe actors, Bellan, playing the double role and Sharon Lockwood, as Rose, among others. Their performances were acclaimed by audiences and critics. As Bernard Weiner put it, 'It's rare to find comic ensemble playing on this level. Lockwood is a delight ... Bellan generates laughs even when silent. Both are masters of comic timing.' (Weiner, 1985) Together with the cast, the setting and the direction were similarly praised, as in the following review: 'Peggy Snider's sets are a major contribution to making this production such a total triumph and Seyd's inventiveness in stage business is breathtaking' (Esta, 1985).

Leo Stutzin wrote: 'The crackling cast and direction do make the theater rock with laughter for two frantic and fast-moving hours. They also force a viewer to think about the assertions, and that is success enough' (Stutzin, 1985: 15). In other words, he seems to indicate that the production, as well as entertaining audiences, managed to make them reflect. Interestingly enough, when the same production was staged in New York two years later, it had mixed reviews. While Marilyn Stasio argued that 'thanks to Richard Seyd's well-controlled maniacally funny production, the political point never gets lost' (Stasio, 1987), Jonathan Kalb wrote

---

[36] Telephone interview with Joan Holden, May 2004.

that the production failed to stimulate the audience's 'political sensibilities' despite a funny and speakable translation (Kalb, 1987). Seyd, like others, believes that this was due to the previously mentioned New York critics' approach towards political theatre, 'they come to it with an attitude, with the idea that they are not going to like it',[37] in Seyd's words. This would explain the differences between the critical reception and the audience's reaction – as happened for the Broadway production of *Accidental Death of an Anarchist* – and the fact that spectators enjoyed the perfomance, as emphasised by Seyd.

Furthermore, it is useful to note that the American première of *About Face* had been staged in 1983 by the Yale Repertory Theatre, New Haven, in an 'English version' by Dale McAdoo and Charles Mann, directed by Andrei Belgrader. This version, based on the 1981 Italian text, is characterised by vulgar language, used in particular by Rosa, the addition and cutting of a number of scenes and the replacement of the *Internazionale* song with *Ave Maria, gratia plena*. It also reproduces the British version in certain parts. Alisa Salomon, among others, argued that the Yale production succeedeed in theatrical terms but not as a political performance: 'This production, directed by Andrei Belgrader, succeeds as an amusing, at times side-splitting farce. It is funny, quick-paced, and generally well-performed. But it does little to shake up American audiences' notions of the machinations of capitalism, the power of money, government, terrorism' (Salomon, 1983a: 64). Once again, as in the case of other plays, the fact that the Eureka production succeeded where others failed appears to confirm the validity of the Eureka approach.

According to Mimi D'Aponte, the Eureka Theatre stagings of Fo's plays are an example of Fo's impact on political theatre. In her overview of the role of Fo's theatre in the United States, she claims that a renewed interest in political theatre and the new form of clowning of the 'New Vaudevillians' were partly the result of Fo's impact. To support her first claim, she mentions Eureka Theatre's stagings of Fo plays and the fact that the company was granted federal funds in 1988. In relation to the second issue, she refers to Hoyle as the leading actor in the above-mentioned production of *Accidental Death of an Anarchist*, and bases her argument on interviews with two American actors who claim that Hoyle was influenced by Fo. Furthermore, as Robert Hurwitt argues, it is thanks to a tradition of mixing comedy with politics, represented by the San Francisco Mime Troupe, that actors, directors and audiences were prepared 'to make the most of Fo' (Hurwitt, 1998). This is also the opinion of Seyd who believes that the critical response to Fo and Rame's work in San Francisco is positively affected by a powerful combination of factors: the political theatre of the San Francisco Mime Troupe, the fact that the 'New Vaudeville' was born there and that San Francisco is a left leaning city. This is why, according to Seyd, San Francisco critics, as opposed to New York critics, 'understand political theatre, they judge a political play on its merit'.[38]

---

[37] Telephone interview, June 2004.
[38] Ibid.

For all the above reasons, San Francisco appears a unique area for the stagings of Fo and Rame's plays. This was further confirmed by the 1998 'FoFest. A celebration of the Art and Work of Dario Fo and Franca Rame', organised by Suzanne Cowan and supported by directors, actors and translators who had beeen involved in stagings of Fo and Rame's work, such as Seyd, Taccone and Jenkins. The Coordinating Committee started by holding a competition for drama students who were asked to adapt and perform Fo and Rame's plays, but when news of the performance and auditions started to circulate, apart from actors and directors, others expressed their interest in the event and volunteered to work on photography, publicity, and fundraising, among other things. The festival was in fact a volunteer event and all artists involved donated their time. The originally planned three events became a six-week multisite celebration, which included six live performances, a video and film series, a panel discussion focusing on the problems of translating Fo and Rame's work for American audiences, exhibits, literature sales and distribution and a hands-on commedia dell'arte workshop. The events were held in a number of venues, including the Museo ItaloAmericano, the Istituto Italiano di Cultura, La Peña Cultural Center. The festival had a good press coverage and each event was sold out. As explained in the programme:

> The event was a source of enlightenment as well as entertainment, and allowed many people to become acquainted with Fo and Rame's work for the first time. More than that, it was a fitting tribute to two brilliant artists who, after a nearly forty-year theatrical career, continue devoting their boundless creative energies to struggle against all forms of injustice, oppression, and official stupidity.

Such a unique event, described by the organizers as 'the world's first festival entirely devoted to a celebration of the art and work of this extraordinary couple', would seem a long-waited compensation for so many unfortunate productions on the East Coast.

Chapter 5

Fo and Rame's Theatre Today

This final chapter engages in discussions of what staging Fo and Rame's political theatre means in the twenty-first century. Productions of Fo and Rame classics, such as the 2003 Scottish staging of *Mistero Buffo* and West End production of *Accidental Death of an Anarchist* in the same year, seem to indicate that dominant translation strategies, analysed in previous chapters, continue to affect the British approach to their theatre. Other performances, instead, such as the 2001 American première of *Johan Padan and the Discovery of the Americas*, demonstrate that it is possible to encourage a new approach to Fo and Rame's theatre, whereby rewriters challenge their audiences and infuse new life into this subcategory of the theatrical system.

The 2003 British productions of *Mistero Buffo* and *Accidental Death of an Anarchist* share two central aspects. First, the tendency to a predominantly comic and safe reading of Italian theatre which still appears to be very strong. Second, such stagings function as showcases for well-known comic actors, namely Andy Gray and Rhys Ifans. Interestingly enough, despite such similarities, the production of *Mistero Buffo* was negatively received while *Accidental Death of an Anarchist* was incredibly successful. At the same time it is worth noticing that the main difference between a British production of Fo and Rame's theatre in 2003 and one in the 1970s and 1980s is that caricaturing stage representations of Italians have disappeared.

Mistero Buffo is Fo's most successful one-man show and it consists of a series of *giullarate*, individual pieces, in *grammelot*. Fo has defined *grammelot* as a 'sproloquio onomatopeico', an onomatopoeic goobledygook which reproduces the phonetics of foreign languages and dialects, and includes a limited number of existing words (Fo, 1997a: 89). As Fo argues, it was a theatrical technique used by Italian comic actors working abroad to overcome the language barriers. It was thanks to a combination of *grammelot* with comic gags, so-called *lazzi*, that they could successfully perform abroad. Similarly, Fo creates *grammelot* imitating foreign languages, such as French and English. As he explains in his *Manuale minimo dell'attore*, Fo improvises following the phonetics of a given language and from time to time he adds common words, such as 'yes' in English, which give the impression that he is speaking that language. Each *giullarata* in *Mistero Buffo* is preceded by a prologue, in which Fo establishes a direct dialogue with his audience and narrates the story that he will be performing. The prologues introducing the *giullarate* make the dramatic text secondary to Fo's kinetic language. This is why *Mistero Buffo* is accessible to audiences of all nationalities and it explains why it is the work that Fo often performs abroad. Defined by Fo as a grotesque spectacle, *Mistero Buffo* takes irreverent and comic aspects of mystery plays and narrates biblical legends from the point of view of common people. For example, the miracle of Cana is told from two competing perspectives, that of the archangel who provides the official version of the miracle and and that of a drunken man who focuses on the enjoyment derived from the miracle. In other words, the human dimension of the stories, based on a number of medieval sources, is more central than the religious context. Unsurprisingly, *Mistero Buffo*, particularly the piece on Pope Boniface VIII emphasising the contrast between the poverty preached by Jesus and the luxurious life conducted by the Pope, has been condemned by the Vatican as blasphemous.

The prologues allow Fo to break the fourth wall and to engage the audience by introducing satirical references to current political events. Such direct dialogues with the audience are distinct from the *giullarate* and at the same time constitute an integral part of the overall show. While the individual pieces focus on biblical and medieval events and are in grammelot, the prologues, which are in Italian, take the spectator outside the historical context of the performance and introduce a contemporary frame of reference. It is the combination of these two parts of the show and the subsequent interlocking of two parallel dimensions, linking past and present, that makes *Mistero Buffo* politically challenging. The prologues are funny and entertaining like the *giullarate* following them precisely because of Fo's ability in contextualising political satire by lampooning powerful figures. When Fo performs *Mistero Buffo* abroad or when the play is translated and staged in other languages, the prologues serve precisely to draw similarities between medieval cases of oppression and local examples of injustice and to introduce contemporary social issues.

The Borderline production of *Mistero Buffo*, directed by Gerard Kelly, toured Scotland from April to May 2003. Borderline is a well-known Scottish touring theatre company, which has often appeared at the Edinburgh Fringe Festival. This production was based on Fullarton and Farrell's adaptation, but, as indicated in the programme, it included additional material by David Cosgrove. The following pieces from *Mistero Buffo* were staged: *The Raising of Lazarus*, *The Marriage Feast at Cana*, *The Blind Man and The Cripple* and *Pope Boniface VIII*. While Gray's talent was praised by some, the critical response to the overall production was rather negative. The review appeared in the *Scotsman*, for example, entitled 'Satire should be ruthless not toothless' criticised the production for reducing the play to 'easy, depoliticised humour' and for lacking 'political punch'. More precisely Mark Brown wrote: 'This isn't satirical clowning so much as music-hall Fo. Kelly and Gray have pulled the satirist's teeth' (2003). Moreover, Joyce McMillan argued that *Mistero Buffo* seemed to be out of time:

> For no matter how powerfully these stories are told, the fact is that in our secular north European society, where Catholicism has not been the faith of the establishment for centuries, mocking the lies and pomposities of the church is no longer news – if it ever

was – and it would take a far more radical and thorough updating than this gentle effort, lightly directed by Gerard Kelly, to make these stories work for us. The show looks good, on a glittery chat-show set by Geoff Rose, and Gray's rapport with the audience is always a joy to watch. But for now, Mistero Buffo seems like a show out of time; a huge theatrical talent focuses on the wrong script at the wrong moment. (McMillan, 2003).

The critic's remark appears to confirm that Borderline failed to make the play relevant for domestic audiences, also because the prologues were filled with superficial and banal references to contemporary British and Scottish politics.

In this sense it is worth noticing that, as Farrell argues, rather than translating the prologues of *Mistero Buffo*, new introductions need to be specially rewritten and addressed to local audiences, as he and Morag Fullarton did when they adapted Ed Emery's translation in 1990 (Farrell, 1990: 12). For example, among other things, Farrell and Fullarton rewrote the prologue to *The Marriage Feast at Cana* to emphasise the contemporary resonances that drinking has in Scotland as a theological and social problem. Furthermore, one of the main obstacles in staging *Mistero Buffo* outside Italy is mantaining the historical perspective inherent to Fo's satire on political and social issues. In other words, as Farrell puts it (1990), since *Mistero Buffo* draws on the Italian tradition of the *giullare*, it becomes paramount to link stagings of the play in other languages with local theatrical traditions. This was the strategy behind Robbie Coltrane's performance in the 1990 Borderline Theatre Company touring production of *Mistero Buffo*, based on Farrell and Fullarton's adaptation, which was also broadcast on BBC 2. In Mitchell's words, Coltrane succeeded in creating 'engaging, entertaining theatre entirely in the spirit of Fo's original' (Mitchell, 1990: 44).[1] The 2003 production instead, rather than drawing attention to local issues through a political satire rooted in history, appears to have undermined the parallel between past and present and to have inserted safe and obvious political allusions to George Bush, Tony Blair, and George Galloway, among others. As Brown put it:

> It is unforgivable to reduce it to the easy, depoliticised humour of this offering. The piece rose to fame in Italy for its biting use of Bible stories to assault the pillars of the contemporary establishment, but here Andy Gray has to make an early acknowledgement of criticisms that this touring presentation lacks political punch. Trying to remedy that shortcoming by attaching tired, safe references to Archer and Portillo only highlights the fact he and Gerard Kelly have missed the point. (Brown, 2003)

---

[1] Borderline, together with the above-mentioned 1990 production of *Mistero Buffo*, has successfully produced a number of Fo's plays, such as *Trumpets and Raspberries* in 1985 and 1995, *The Virtuous Burglar* and *An Ordinary Day* in 1988, *Can't Pay? Won't Pay!* in 1990.

It is interesting to note that these were exactly the same accusations brought against the 1984 Broadway production of *Accidental Death of an Anarchist*, which caused the show's flop.

The West End production of *Accidental Death of an Anarchist*, staged at the Donmar Warehouse Theatre, from February to April 2003, directed by Robert Delamere, was instead praised as 'a smashing production' based on Simon Nye's 'sparky new translation'.[2] The title page of the programme is dominated by an image of a bomb fuse, drawing audience's attention more to the terrorist issue of placing bombs, rather than to police corruption. There are a number of quotations by well known writers on justice and anarchism, one next to the other, including the following: (1) 'Usually terrible things that are done with the excuse that progress requires them, are not really progress at all, but just terrible things.' (Russell Baker); (2) 'Laws are like sausages, it is better not to see them being made.' (Otto Van Bismarck); (3) 'In the absence of justice, what is sovereignty, but organised robbery?' (Saint Augustine); (4) 'Anarchism is a game at which the police can beat you' (Bernard Shaw); (5) 'Laughter should open the mind of the audience so that the nails of reason can be hammered in' (Molière) and last but not least Dario Fo's statement in large letters: 'Forgetfulness is the world's most dangerous disease.'

Simon Nye is the author of the award-winning sitcom *Men Behaving Badly*, among other things, as well as a translator and a writer. He has translated Molière's *Don Juan*, staged in Bristol in October 2002. Interestingly enough, in the published text we read: 'This new translation by playwright and screenwriter Simon Nye is faithful to the Italian version' (Fo, 2003). Nye's article in the *Guardian* allows us to have a detailed description of the strategy informing this production. Nye makes a distinction between his version and Richards' s 1979 version of the play:

> Not so much a translation, more a rumbustious approximation, it was a crowd-pleasing rollercoaster. These days Fo isn't quite as keen on the (as it were) circus-isation of his work, so the Donmar's and my own more radical ideas were vetoed. I still passionately believe that a mime version set in war-torn Guernsey would have worked, but theatre folk can be very cautious. At the suggestion of the director, Robert Delamere, we have relocated the play to contemporary Britain. (Nye, 2003)

In this sense the production adheres to the strategy of relocating foreign plays to British contexts, which has become very common, and it does so in a number of ways.

To start with, the Maniac enters dressed as Spiderman and the audience laughs immediately both because of his persona and his costume. A Spiderman routine goes on for some time and, together with a number of farcical scenes added in the performance, contributes from the very beginning to undermine the radical satire of the play. The scene where the Maniac, alone in the police office, answers the

---

[2]Programme of *Accidental Death of an Anarchist*, Donmar Warehouse Theatre, 2003.

phone pretending to be the Inspector is much longer and a number of other comic routines are exaggerated. At one point a bunch of flowers falls from the ceiling as a tribute to the Maniac. When the Maniac argues that 'scandal is the fertilizer of democracy' the audience is too busy laughing at the Inspector's silly gestures to take in one of the central points of the play. Towards the end, the Maniac, who often changes clothes on the stage when switching from one impersonation to another, is naked between one change of costumes and another.

There are a number of cultural clichés inserted in the performance, but not in the translated text. For example, the Maniac uses a French accent when he talks about his role as a psychiatrist and impersonates a stereotypical French man. He also plays the role of the gay man quite heavily, despite the fact that there is only one stage direction suggesting that the actor plays camp. He even embodies the stereotype of the terrorist with a red scarf on his head. The reference to Italian punctuation and grammar is substituted with one to the Welsh language in the performance, but not in the text, and references are made to Scottish rabbit and cows. The language of the translation is often rather vulgar, a point in common with Richards's version and even the choice of music and songs contributes to the 'circus-isation' of the play. In the Italian text the Maniac fools the police into singing an anarchist song, here there is a rap atmosphere when they sing *Don't Believe the Hype* by Public Enemy. Pop music songs are sung, such as *Stop the Children*. And after the interval, they sing and play country music as well as singing the National Anthem.

The combination of Nye's translation with the director and actors' choices have produced a performance text which is built on a series of cultural stereotypes, farcical scenes and physical comedy. Most important of all, this affects the representation of the police characters. Nye's comments on this issue are fascinating:

> If you leave the play in its original setting, there is a risk that the evening gets caught between satirising and paying tribute to the Italian fashions of the late 1960s. The play is about the murder of an innocent man, not how amusing bushy sideburns and large Sophia Loren-style glasses now look. The vanity and swagger of the Italian carabinieri visibly delighting in their pristine uniforms, has always been shocking. The British police have a less sensual relationship with their uniforms. (…) I have never seen a British policeman in sunglasses, whereas I imagine they're still pretty damn de rigueur down the Appian Way. Italian police also invariably carry a gun, which gives you that special edge if you're serious about your swaggering. (ibid.)

Nye undeniably contradicts himself by first arguing that the play has nothing to do with clichés about Italian culture and then dedicating a whole paragraph of his article to the stereotypical image of Italian policemen. He then goes on by arguing that *Accidental Death* remains intensely Italian, despite having contemporary resonances, such as terrorism. He even argues that 'Fo brilliantly mocks the disorganised nature of much of the anarchist threat: after all, a hyper-efficient anarchist machine doesn't seem quite right.' Nye here makes a superficial reading of the play arguing that it has contemporary resonance because it mocks anarchist terrorism. Fo does not mock the nature of anarchism in the play; on the contrary he reveals the falsity of police accusation and their cover up.

It is worth remembering that in the introduction to the first edition of the play, Fo argued that *Accidental Death of an Anarchist* was an accusation against la 'strage di stato', state massacre, and the murder of Pinelli. In Fo's view, theatre is a political tool that should allow a critical understanding and awareness of history and class struggle. Interestingly enough, Nye argues:

> It is a vital function of theatre, indeed art and entertainment generally, that figures of authority should occasionally be ridiculed. And Fo ridicules. Of course, the risk of satirising dubious police officers on stage is that they come across as merely buffoonish, rather than the kind of men who would beat someone to death in a cell or push an innocent man out of a window. The officers in Accidental Death need to generate laughter, but also fear. (ibid.)

This is precisely the most important aspect of the play, as previously argued, and while Nye seems to be aware of it, his translation, together with the director and actors' interpretation of the play, achieve very different results. This mixture of a partial misunderstanding of the play combined with specific stage choices, has succeeded in making audiences laugh, rather than making them feel uncomfortable, as Fo wishes to do with his theatre. Nye concludes his article by arguing that 'Fo's plays don't bother to coax the average Daily Mail reader across the political divide. What they do offer is the theatrical equivalent of being laughed into bed.'

Needless to say, apart from Nye's strategy to relocate the play as opposed to Richards's use of stereotypical images of Italian culture in the 1979 staging, the similarities between the two productions are striking. Nye makes Richards's double ending even more extreme and has the audience vote as if it were a TV show:

> Maniac: Oh yes, my bomb. Now, this being a country with a fetish for voting as demonstrated by the TV show Big Brother and rather less convincingly by the Prime Minister's show Big Parliamentary Elections – I am going to allow you to vote on whether I blow up this stinking cesspit of a police station with its free gift, as it were, of one power-mad, muckraking pussy-power journalist. So please get out your mobile phones and turn them on. (Fo, 2003: 86)

The stage direction reads that a gameshow-style board with two telephone numbers drops down, while Bertozzo, the Superintendent and the journalist try and persuade the audience to vote for them, and the Maniac wanders among the audience to check if they are voting. In Nye's version not only blowing up the police becomes part of the play, the audience is encouraged even further to get involved in this terrorist attack. Interestingly enough, this TV style voting does not happen in the performance. Then this version follows the ending of the first edition of *Accidental Death of an Anarchist* and the actor playing the Maniac comes back on stage as the real judge.

The well-known actor Rhys Ifans (who starred in the successful movie *Notting Hill*) playing the Maniac was one of the main focuses of attention. But while his incredible performance was unanimously praised and contributed to the success of the production, the same cannot be said for the leading actor in *Mistero Buffo*. As emphasised in the press, the staging was a showcase for Gray more than anything else. A one-man show such as *Mistero Buffo* by definition requires a talented actor and at the same time it is one of the best opportunities for an actor to put his acting skills on display. While Gray had previously performed in three of Fo's plays, this was his first one-man show. In McMillan's view, the focus on Gray's skills as a well-known comic actor, who had just played in the incredibly successful *Art* at the Royal Lyceum, inevitably affected the staging since his performance pushed the play even more towards safe and superficial satire (McMillan, 2003). It was even argued that

> The production is forced to treat political satire as an optional extra because this is, in fact, all about Gray. Everything, from the glaikit, Glaswegian characterisations to the physical comedy (more panto than farce), is tailored to the comic actor's public persona. He is, without question, a real talent. The great pity is that he has opted to play it safe when he has the opportunity to exhibit his range. (Brown, 2003)

As previously shown, the choice to star a famous actor in British stagings of foreign plays is not uncommon, in the same way as it is not uncommon to have foreign texts adapted by a well-known playwright or director.[3] But the negative critical response to the 2003 staging of *Mistero Buffo* confirms the prestige of the first Scottish production of the play to which Gray's performance was compared. Directly and indirectly, critics and audiences based their interpretation of Gray's acting on their knowledge of Coltrane's *Mistero Buffo*. This, combined with David Cosgrove's intervention on Fullarton and Farrell's adaptation, affected the production and prevented it from being politically effective, as previous Scottish stagings were.

Let us now move to the most recent American production of *Accidental Death of an Anarchist* revealing a different approach from the British staging. Jenkins's new translation was staged in a co-production by the Dallas Theater Center with the Pittsburgh Public Theater, directed by the Dallas Theater Center Artistic Director Richard Hamburger. After previews in January 2004, the production moved to Pittsburgh from March to April, where it was also staged as part of the

---

[3] In 1998 Peter Hall directed a production of Eduardo De Filippo's *Filumena*, translated by the dramatist Timberlake Wertenbaker, at the Piccadilly Theatre, starring Judy Dench and Michael Pennington. The combination of Hall, Wertenbaker and Dench's names, stars of the British theatrical system, ensured the incredible success of De Filippo's play.

18th Annual Pittsburgh Public Theater Benefit for the Pittsburgh Aids Task Force. Co-productions have obvious financial advantages as well as giving the actors more time to work on the play and allowing larger audiences to see it. As the director argued: 'It opens up fresh ideas to each theater in terms of different styles of working. The actors also get to work on two different kinds of stages, ours, a proscenium, and then on a thrust stage, in Pittsburgh' (quoted in Lowry, 2004a).

Furthermore, Jenkins consulted with Fo and Rame for the translation, as well as collaborating with the director and the actors during rehearsals. One of the most relevant decisions was to keep the original 1970s Italian setting, as Holden had also done for the 1984 Eureka Theatre production. This was Jenkins's and the director's choice with Fo and Rame's approval. Most important of all, Jenkins aimed at making it clear that 'The loss of civil liberties in the interest of national security and the illegal detention of citizens that happened in Italy in 1970 is clearly parallel to what is happening now in America as a result of September 11, the war in Iraq and the fear created by President Bush about national security.'[4]

Among other things, the leading actor and the director added a short prologue in which the Maniac ironically disavows the applicability of the staged events to an American context. This prologue reinforces the above-mentioned parallels which it seems to be denying in the same way as the prologue of the first Italian edition of the play.

> The play was written in Italy over thirty years ago and any resemblance to the United States is purely coincidental. Anarchy could never happen in America. For instance kicking an elected governor out of office and replacing him with an Austrian body builder whose claim to fame is portraying a vengeful robot in the movies might seem like anarchism, but it's not. That's just Hollywood. The anarchist referred to in this play, Giuseppe Pinelli, was actually killed in a fall from a 5th story window while in police custody in 1969 in Milano, but you shouldn't let that upset you. Things like that never could happen in America. We would never allow the police to kill a man arrested for a crime he didn't commit. That's what the death penalty's for. Just kidding.

As Richard Hamburger argues, while the production is set in an Italian police station, it is through the prologue and thanks to the Maniac that similarities between Italy and the United States are pointed out. The Maniac, in particular, moves through time and space and while making the audience laugh he stimulates them to reflect on their own social and political context.[5] Moreover, rather than adding explicit and obvious references to American politics, Jenkins makes specific translation choices which bring audiences to make those connections for themselves. For example, when the Maniac is asked if he has ever impersonated a judge, he admits that he has never had the opportunity but that he would love to be

---

[4] Telephone interview with Ron Jenkins, December 2003.
[5] Telephone interview with Richard Hamburger, November 2004.

a 'giudice di cassazione' at least once. The change of the Italian 'Appeal Court' to 'Supreme Court' judge, immediately makes spectators think of the American Supreme Court and the 2000 elections. Or, as Elaine Liner argues, by keeping the expression 'scandals should be invented even when there aren't any, because it keeps the leaders in power' as it is, 'the name Monica Lewinsky shuffles forward on the mental Rolodex' (Liner, 2004).

Liner's following comments about the Dallas preview, among several positive reviews, indicate that the production has succeeded in making the play relevant to contemporary American audiences while being funny:

> The test of any play's greatness, particularly one so grounded in particular events in time, is its ability to remain relevant. Anarchist certainly does that. Allowing for updates, the script stays fluid. … Comedy, according to Dario Fo, can be an incentive to political action, a weapon against the falsehoods and bloated platitudes of the high and mighty. It's scary how true the messages in Anarchist still are 30 years after it was written. (Liner, 2004)

Ted Hoover in *The Pittsburgh City Paper* described the play as follows: 'Outrageous jokes, unbelievably goofy characters, the obliteration of the fourth wall: Fo does it all with the deft hand of a master farceur, but with an acid-etched purpose', adding that 'the new translation/adaptation by Ron Jenkins … amazingly, one-ups Fo at his own game' (Hoover, 2004). Hamburger's direction and the casting were also praised. According to Mark Lowry, 'Richard Hamburger has assembled a fabulous cast who handle the slapstick physical comedy and whirleybird wordplay effortlessly. As the impersonation-crazed Maniac, Robert Dorfman proves himself a comic genius' (Lowry, 2004b).

Jenkins was also responsible for the 2001 American première of *Johan Padan and the Discovery of the Americas*, based on his translation, which confirms his commitment to making the social and political significance of Fo and Rame's plays resonate with American audiences. *Johan Padan* was staged with Tommy Derrah, under Jenkins's direction, at the American Repertory Theater, Cambridge, the Provincetown Playhouse in New York, at the Wesleyan Center for the Arts, Middletown, Connecticut and then at the International Festival of Arts and Ideas in New Haven in 2001. The première at the ART was part of a festival to celebrate the 50th anniversary of Fo and Rame's theatrical career. The festival was supposed to include 10 nights from 20 September of Fo and Rame performing their respective signature one-person shows, *Mistero Buffo* and *Sex? Thanks, Don't Mind If I Do!* But because of September 11th, Fo and Rame decided not to travel to the United States and to cancel their performances since they believed that given the circumstances the time was not appropriate for them to perform.

Johan Padan is a peasant character, a man of the mountains, who tells his audience how, despite the fact that he does not like sailing, he became a stowaway on Christopher Columbus's boat to escape the Inquisition. When he gets to America, he is made prisoner by a tribe of cannibals, but due to a series of circumstances the cannibals end up believing that he is a healer and he is named 'figlio del sol che nasce', son of the rising sun. He is also forced to teach Catechism to the Indians. In the end he encourages and organizes a Native American insurrection. Johan's narration of the discovery of America and his personal experience constitute a provocative and irreverent version of historical events, typical of Fo's theatre. As Fo writes in the preface: 'First of all, you should know that this is not a woeful tale of the Indian massacres perpetrated by the Conquistadors. And it is not the usual story of a defeated race. On the contrary, it is an epic chronicle of Indians who were victorious' (Fo, 2001: ix).

It is about the discovery of the Americas seen from the perspective of a 'no-tagonist', in Fo's words, representing the experience of all those desperate people who are ignored in the official history. While Fo documented himself on history books, diaries and autobiographies, as he acknowledges in the prologue, what makes Johan Padan's account unique and hilarious are those scenes which are the result of Fo's imagination. For example, on the way to the Americas the ship on which Johan Padan was travelling was wrecked and he recounts how he survived with other members of the crew by embracing pigs. More precisely, while holding onto the pigs and going under the waves they ended up kissing the animals over and over again:

> After a while the pigs started liking it ... they went under even when there weren't any waves! So the five of us, each embracing his own life-saving animal, and smooching it too ... traversed the thrashing waves that ripped off our shirts and trousers, and we made it to the land ... naked! (Fo, 2001a: 26)

As in the case of all his one-man shows, Fo plays an imaginary cast of hundreds of characters, constantly breaking the fourth wall. Like *Mistero Buffo*, *Johan Padan* is introduced by a prologue which gives Fo the opportunity to address his satire to current political and religious figures and events. More precisely, in Mitchell's words, 'Johan Padan is total theatre on an epic scale in which Fo confronts issues of colonialism, imperialism, cultural plurality, freedom, scatology, sex, the supernatural, laughter and the grotesque and displays his most complex and sustained performative achievement' (1999: 215).

As he writes in his preface to the published translation, Jenkins spent some weeks with Fo and Rame in Italy while working on the first rough translation. On that occasion Fo performed most of the text for Jenkins and by doing so he provided the translator with a clear image of the physicality embedded in his text. Jenkins started working as onstage simultaneous translator for both Fo and Rame in 1986 and through that experience he has learned the connection between the musicality of Fo's words and the kinetic language of his body. As Jenkins argues:

> Watching him read small portions of the text at his home reaffirmed the intricacy of its physical details. The sounds of the words were charged with a physical memory ... Fo was remembering the text the way he had written it, with his body and I have tried to

translate it the same way, with sensitivity to the kinetic and pictorial origins of the story, and with hopes that readers may occasionally have the urge to dance out a few passages with their fingers. (Fo, 2001a: viii)

Jenkins's attention to Fo's kinetic style, both when translating and directing his plays, represents a refreshing approach to Fo's theatre, which rather than focusing on the comic quality of his plays, takes into account the complex physical rhythms of his texts.

Furthermore, Jenkins decided to project some of Fo's colourful paintings as a backdrop for Derrah's performance. As in several other cases, Fo made numerous paintings about the story of Johan Padan's encouter with the new world and then wrote the monologue on the basis of these pictures. In Jenkins's words:

The words came out of the pictures, inseparable from the actions and the movements that he used to tell the story. So the piece was born in a kinetic way. Tommy is a wonderfully kinetic actor, so he understands instinctively that you don't just talk the language, you evoke it with the whole body.

Derrah, who had performed *The Story of the Tiger*, analysed in the previous chapter, created his own acting style to interpret Fo's monologue without exaggerating its comic aspects or adopting any particular accent. Derrah aimed at reproducing the cinematic quality of those drawings constantly providing new perspectives through his body and his voice. Spectators were very responsive and participated with enthusiasm in the discussion following the show. In particular, the discussion that took place in Middletown on 17 September 2001 indicated that the audience enjoyed the performance because it was based on a physical acting technique, in the *commedia dell'arte* style, which involves a direct relationship with the audience. Interestingly enough, spectators commented that they appreciated this kind of theatre precisely because they were not accustomed to seeing it very often.

Terry Byrne in his review of the American Repertory Theatre production also praised Derrah's interpretation of the play:

On a bare stage, dressed in a long-sleeved T-shirt and jeans, Derrah conjures a world that is rich in imagery, full of sound and fury with enormous energy and physical agility. ... Although Derrah consistently delivers the goods in whatever role he takes on, 'Johan Padan' seems to bring together all of his comic skills and enrich them with some serious breadth and depth. ... Derrah's achievement is that he captures the essence of Fo's politically charged comedy without having to imitate him. (Byrne, 2001)

Byrne's response to *Johan Padan* was very different from previous reactions to Fo's plays in that the argument that Fo's theatre cannot be staged in the United States because of American acting style is turned upside down. This time the critic did not praise the performance as a compensation for the shortcomings of the source play; on the contrary he argued that *Johan Padan* enriches Derrah's comic skills.

The above-mentioned productions of *Johan Padan* and *Accidental Death of an Anarchist* share a political resonance thanks to Jenkins's approach to Fo and Rame's theatre. They subvert those American stage traditions that tend to focus on the cultural identity of foreign plays. Most important of all, they confirm that a response to Fo and Rame's plays based on a careful choice of staging strategies, particularly the acting style, produces coherent performance texts, whose cultural origins are minimised rather than made predominant. In this sense, they represent significant examples of theatre as intercultural exchange, as identified by David Johnston. Johnston argues that in the era of new technologies when tribalism is a growing response to the perceived dangers of globalisation, theatre has the opportunity 'not only to suggest the interstices between cultures, but also to enable their proper functioning as spaces for exchange. ... It is this perspective, central to both theatre and translation, this hint of a new life-enriching and culturally-enabling power, which might be most legitimately felt to be genuinely intercultural' (Johnston, 2000: 13, 21).

Conclusion

While I was writing the conclusions to this book a new comedy written by and starring Fo and Rame, *Anomalo bicefalo* opened in Rome on 1 of December 2003 and toured throught Italy. *Anomalo bicefalo* is a satire against the Italian prime minister Silvio Berlusconi and the political, financial, media system he has created, which dominates every aspect of Italian life. The title refers to the surreal story in which Berlusconi and the Russian Putin fall victim to a terrorist attack during a recent conference of surgeons specialising in organ transplants, held in Sicily. While Putin dies, Berlusconi can be saved thanks to an operation which replaces Berlusconi's damaged brain with the sane parts of Putin's brain. The Italian Prime Minister becomes a two brained 'anomalous' human being. More precisely, he is a dwarf played by Fo and an invisible mime. The story is narrated through a job interview to a charismatic lady, played by Rame, in a television set. Rame also plays the Prime Minister's wife, Veronica Lario. Several Italian politicians are mocked on stage, including left-wing ex-ministers, such as Massimo D'Alema who appears as a puppet.

There have been several attempts at censoring the play starting from the board of the Milan Piccolo Teatro. Other theatre managers requested to read the text before putting it on stage, but Fo and Rame refused to let them read it. This created an intense debate in the media, also due to the fact that the television performances of a number of satirists, such as Paolo Rossi and Sabina Guzzanti, had been subject to censorship. In the end *Anomalo bicefalo* was not censored, but Fo and Rame were sued for defamation by a Forza Italia politician Marcello Dell'Utri demanding one million euros as compensation because the show makes references to his alleged links with the mafia, despite the fact that Dell'Utri was under investigation precisely for this reason. As a consequence the play was first broadcast on the cable television channel Sky with no sound. As Rame argued when I recently interviewed her, 'Dobbiamo ringraziare il Cda del Piccolo per la grande pubblicità gratuita che ci ha fatto. In tutte le città c'è già il tutto esaurito! La situazione è identica al periodo di *Canzonissima* quando il Vaticano si scagliò contro *Mistero Buffo*' (Rame, 2004: 21).[1]

The reaction provoked by the performance seems to confirm *Anomalo bicefalo*'s political function. It is a play which makes you laugh while denouncing

---

[1] 'We should thank the board of the Piccolo for all the free publicity they have given us. It is sold out everywhere. It is exactly what happened at the time of *Canzonissima* when the Vatican condemned *Mistero Buffo*.'

the frightening political and social decay of contemporary Italy under Berlusconi's government. In a country now marked by censorhip and repressive laws, *Anomalo bicefalo* indicates that Fo and Rame's political satire continues to offer opportunities for public debates and social critique. Fo has explained the need to write such a play: 'Non faccio l'eroe, è una questione di impegno. Abbiamo alle spalle cinquant'anni di teatro militante, la gente si aspetta che non molliamo proprio ora' (quoted in Anselmi, 2003).[2]

Gianfranco Capitta, among others, wrote a positive review in *Il Manifesto* arguing that 'ci si arrabbia e si ride, moltissimo, in sala come sul palcoscenico' (2003: 15).[3] But it should be noted that the critical response was not so encouraging in terms of the play's dramatic structure. In Enrico Groppali's view, *Anomalo bicefalo* 'non è una farsa. Non è nemmeno una satira politica stesa in forma drammatica' (Groppali, 2003).[4] Michele Anselmi defines the play as a 'dramma sarcastico, invero pencolante più verso l'avanspettacolo che la farsa' (Anselmi, 2003).[5] In other words, *Anomalo bicefalo* appears to be politically relevant but not theatrically effective. The lack of a coherent dramatic structure turns it into a kind of variety theatre. Interestingly enough, as previously shown, similar reservations had been expressed in relation to the dramatic nature of other Fo and Rame's plays never staged in English.

If we relate this with the fact that the majority of Fo and Rame's latest plays, with the exception of *Johan Padan*, are completely unknown in English-speaking countries, the complexity and contradictions inherent to British and American stagings of Fo and Rame's plays, as shown throughout this book, become apparent. The same plays, written in the 1970s, translated and performed in the United Kingdom and the United States in the late 1970s and 1980s, continue to be translated and staged in the twenty-first century. This is testified by the 2003 productions of *Mistero Buffo* and *Accidental Death of an Anarchist*, analysed in the last chapter. Despite Fo being awarded the Nobel Prize, and despite common claims that he is the world's most performed playwright, we need to recognise that the knowledge and the images of Fo and Rame's theatre outside Italy have been affected by the limited number of plays which have been translated and staged.

On the one hand, the emphasis on Fo and Rame's most successful plays dating back to the 1970s, at the expense of other theatre texts written since then, testifies to a tendency among British and American rewriters to play safe and to rely on those plays which have established Fo and Rame's reputation. *Accidental Death of an Anarchist*, as argued in chapter four, boasts a unique record as a foreign play, that of being on stage in the West End for two consecutive years. Such a record makes it very appealing to British directors while other unknown plays are

---

[2] 'I am not acting as a hero, it is a matter of commitment. We have done militant theatre for fifty years, people expect us not to give up right now.'
[3] 'One gets angry and laughs a lot, in the house as well as on stage.'
[4] 'It is not a farce. It is not a political satire in dramatic form either.'
[5] 'A biting drama, tending more towards burlesque rather than farce.'

neglected. On the other hand, one further reason why Fo and Rame's more recent plays are not translated and staged abroad may be that some of them, like *Anomalo bicefalo*, differ from previous successful plays in theatrical terms. The fact that *Anomalo bicefalo* is not such a well constructed theatre piece would prevent it from being attractive to foreign theatre companies and audiences.

What is even more interesting is that the limited knowledge of Fo and Rame's theatre is far from being an isolated case, since the same applies to a number of foreign playwrights. Seminal figures of twentieth century theatre, such as Luigi Pirandello and Bertolt Brecht, have been subject to a similar destiny since their reputation is also based on a handful of plays. The implications of the contrast between the status of a number of playwrights and the restricted knowledge of their work cannot go unnoticed. Such contrast confirms even further what has been argued in this book, i.e. that Fo and Rame's plays, like other foreign plays, translated into English represent a subcategory within the domestic theatrical system, subject to specific interpreting strategies and staging techniques.

By way of conclusion, I would like to put the reception of Fo and Rame's plays within a broader context, that is the reception of foreign theatre, by briefly comparing it to that of other playwrights. This will indicate the existence of predominant strategies adopted in British and American theatre towards well-known foreign dramatists, besides Fo and Rame. More precisely, the reception of Luigi Pirandello and Garcia Lorca's work represents a further example of the ways in which foreign theatre is put on stage in the United Kingdom and the United States. For a long time since Pirandello's plays were introduced to British audiences in the twenties, they have often been defined as being too cerebral, heavy and doctrinaire. In this sense, it could be argued that Pirandello's theatre has been identified in similar terms as Brecht's theatre. The difficulties of presenting Pirandello to British audiences have been dealt with through two main different strategies. According to one approach, which coincided with the first phase of introduction of Pirandello in the United Kingdom, the Italianness of his plays was emphasised. An opposite strategy, aiming at the Anglicisation and Americanisation of Pirandello's theatre, has equally informed a number of performances in English and interestingly enough, the Anglicised Pirandello has been more appreciated than the Pirandello with all his Italian peculiarities.[6]

The same two strategies have been adopted in response to foreign playwrights of different nationalities, including Lorca. In Nicholas de Jongh's view, the fact that the high poetic diction of Lorca's plays is something that is rarely found in the British repertoire has been the 'prime disincentive to Lorca productions' in the United Kingdom (de Jongh, 1989). Furthermore, David Johnston argues that in some ways Lorca's journey towards otherness, towards alternative expressions of sexuality has been another deterrent, since it can be disturbing for English-

---

[6] See Taviano and Lorch, 2000.

speaking audiences. As a result, and also because of the predominant Stanislavsky based acting style, some British productions of Lorca tend to emphasise its exoticism by inserting flamenco dancing and stage Spanish accents as symbols of the otherness of his plays, in exactly the same way as excessive gesticulating can be used as a representation of Italianness. At the same time, the second strategy, which has become more and more common, seems to suggest, in de Jongh's words (1989), that 'we are on the way to discovering conventions by which to render Lorca in English'. The end of copyright restrictions, combined with the publication of Ian Gibson's biography of Lorca, and with productions that transpose Lorca's work to new contexts relevant to British audiences, are all factors that have contributed to making Lorca one of the most frequently performed foreign dramatists in the eighties and nineties.

The British and American approaches to Pirandello and Lorca, together with the productions of Brecht's plays analysed in the third chapter, demonstrate that common theatrical strategies are adopted in British and American theatre to deal with foreign playwrights. Although neither Pirandello nor Lorca are commonly viewed as political playwrights and despite the considerable differences between their theatre on the one hand and Fo/Rame and Brecht's theatre on the other, the similarities in the reception of their work lay in the fact that numerous productions indicate the British and American theatrical systems' refusal of a provocative approach to theatre which stimulates and disturbs target audiences, rather than reassuring them. Such diverse playwrights have been considered here precisely because the cultural and theatrical diversity of their work seems to confirm common British and American attitudes to foreign theatre, as shown in relation to Fo and Rame's plays.

Having said that, the production of *Johan Padan*, analysed in the previous chapter, shows an attempt to go in a different direction and extend the knowledge of Fo and Rame's theatre by translating and staging unknown plays. Thanks to Jenkins's interest and commitment, *Johan Padan* had a première in English in 2001. The contribution of individuals, playwrights, actors and directors in introducing the work of foreign dramatists to British and American audiences is another important factor that should not be underestimated. As previously indicated, Emery has translated a large number of Fo and Rame's plays and Behan has committed himself to translating unknown plays, such as *Mum's Marijuana*. One can hope that thanks to individuals committed to Fo and Rame even more unknown plays will start to be translated and staged.

This means that British and American stagings of Fo and Rame's theatre provide a complex picture whereby translation strategies analysed in this book, which have been predominant in the British and American theatrical systems for some time, coexist with isolated but nonetheless significant attempts at introducing new ways of staging foreign theatre. Eddershaw in 1996 wondered what the future holds for Brecht and she argued that in order to re-invent Brecht in the United Kingdom, the organisation and structure of British theatre needs to be changed to put an end to the lack of security and long-term employment for actors and to encourage the formation of collective groups. In 2000 Lee Hall's translation of *Mother Courage* was staged at the New Ambassadors Theatre by the London-based Shared Experience, a theatre collective devoted to physical acting. As emphasised in the programme, their work focuses on 'the power and excitement of the performer's physical presence and the unique collaboration between actor and audience' which represents precisely a shared experience, hence the collective's name. They also value the rehearsal process as a vital means to constantly define and 'redefine the possibilities of performance'. The Shared Experience production of *Mother Courage* and the welcoming response that it received seems to support Eddershaw's view that what is required is an approach to theatre that goes beyond the three-week rehearsal period typical of most British productions.

If we consider certain productions of Fo and Rame's plays analysed in the previous chapters, together with the Shared Experience production of *Mother Courage*, it could be argued that a resistant approach has started to emerge. The answer to re-inventing Fo and Rame, together with Brecht, might reside precisely in resistant politics. Furthermore, a radical strategy whereby *Accidental Death of an Anarchist* is changed to *Accidental Death of a Terrorist* and is set in a prison run by American or British forces, such as Guantanamo Bay, would probably be even more politically challenging. In other words, the translator's approach, if combined with the appropriate acting style and staging choices, has the potential to offer a production that paves the way for re-inventing Fo and Rame's theatre in English in line with what Bassnett argues in her essay on Pirandello and translation (Bassnett, 2000). She draws on the view of diverse scholars, such as Barbara Godard and Octavio Paz, to support her image of the translator as somebody who 'liberates the text', who gives a new life to the texts he/she translates. Bassnett suggests to translators to be bold, to undertake the task of translating Pirandello with courage and to 'transpirandellize' the Italian writer to bring his work to life in English.

The productions analysed in this and the previous chapter, far from providing a definite answer to how Fo and Rame's theatre is staged today in the United Kingdom and the United States, suggest that while old translation and stage practices, predominant in the seventies and eighties, have not disappeared, new, challenging strategies are also starting to be adopted. This fact indicates the possible directions that further research in this field might take: more productions of foreign political plays in English-speaking countries need to be studied to examine the relevance and impact of resistant practices in trasposing political theatre across cultures. Particular attention needs to be devoted to acting techniques, the use of theatrical spaces and the interest, or lack of it, in translating unknown political plays and playwrights in English-speaking countries. Studying further the transformation of political theatre beyond cultural and geographical boundaries will contribute to an understanding of the nature and role of political theatre in the twenty-first century. Most important of all, the rewriting of political plays can shed light on the theatrical and cultural frameworks affecting intercultural relations.

Bibliography

A.A.V.V. (1994) *Translation and the (Re)production of Culture*, Selected Papers of the CERA Research Seminars in Translation Studies, 1989-1991. Leuven: CERA Chair for Translation, Communication and Cultures.

Aaltonen, Sirkku (1996a) *Acculturation of the Other. Irish Milieux in Finnish Drama Translation*. Joensuu: Joensuu University Press.

___ (1996b) *Irish milieux in Finnish Drama*. Joensuu: Joensuu University Press.

___ (2000) *Time-Sharing on Stage: Drama Translation in Theatre and Society*. Clevedon: Multilingual Matters.

Abel, Lionel (1963) *Metatheatre, A New View of Dramatic Form*. New York: Hill and Wang.

Ajmone Arsan, Giulia (1987) 'Six Characters at the National Theatre'. *The Yearbook of the British Pirandello Society*, 7, 32-35.

Ali, Tariq (1979) 'Accidental Death of an Anarchist'. *Socialist Challenge*, 12 April, p. 12.

Alter, Jean (1990) *A Sociosemiotic Theory of Theatre*. Philadelphia: University of Pennsylvania Press.

Anonymous (1925a) 'And That's the Truth'. *The Times*, 18 September, p. 15.

___ (1925b) 'Pirandello's Plays'. *The Times Literary Supplement*, 26 March, p. 21.

___ (1958) 'Man, Beast and Virtue'. *The Times*, 9 January, p. 17.

___ (1963) 'Illusion and Reality. Pirandello's Play of Pathos'. *The Times*, 5 April, p. 17.

___ (1965) 'Brecht restored by Berliner Ensemble'. *The Times*, 10 August, p. 16.

___ (1984) Press cutting from the New York Public Library. *New Yorker*, 13 December, pp. 40-43.

Anselmi, Michele (2003) 'Alla prima di L'Anomalo bicefalo'. *Il Giornale*, 5 December, p. 20.

Armistead, Claire (1991) 'Blood Wedding'. *Financial Times*, 19 December, p. 21.

Arnott, Paul (1990) 'Can't Pay! Won't Pay!' *Time Out*, 7 March, p. 29.

Arrowsmith, W., and R. Shattick (eds) (1961) *The Craft and the Context of Translation*. Austin: University of Texas Press.

Ashcroft, Bill, Gareth Griffiths and Helen Tiffin (eds) (1995) *The Post-colonial Studies Reader*. London: Routledge.

Asquith, Ros (1984) 'Mixing the Marxes'. *The Observer*, 18 November, p. 27.

Atkinson, Brooks (1926) 'Midnight Pirandello'. *The New York Times*, 6 December, p. 25.

Auslander, Philip (1992) *Presence and Resistance. Postmodernism and Cultural Politics in Contemporary American Performance*. Ann Arbor: The University of Michigan Press.

Bakhtin, Michael (1968) *Rabelais and His World*. Trans. Helene Iswolsky. Cambridge, MA: MIT Press.

Bandettini, Anna (1989) 'Dario Fo in Vaticano per combattere la droga'. *Repubblica*, 2 November, p. 29.

Banes, Sally (2001) 'Olfactory Performances'. *Tulane Drama Review*, 45.1, 68-76.

Baránski, Zigmunt (1993) 'La diffusione della letteratura italiana contemporanea in Gran Bretagna'. *The Italianist*, 13, 255-265.

Barba, Eugenio (1991) *The Dictionary of Theatre Anthropology: The Secret Art of the Performer*. London: Routledge in association with Centre for Performance Research.

____ (1995) *The Paper Canoe: A Guide to Theatre Anthropology*. Trans. Richard Fowler. London and New York.

Barber, John (1984) 'The Best of Enemies'. *The Daily Telegraph*, 16 November, p. 3.

Barker, Clive (1977) *Theatre Games*. London: Eyre Methuen.

____ (1981) 'Right You Are (If You Could Only Think So)'. *The Yearbook of the British Pirandello Society*, 1, 26-33.

____ (1992) 'Alternative Theatre/Political Theatre'. In Graham Holderness (ed.) *The Politics of Theatre and Drama*. London: Macmillan.

____ (1996) 'The Possibilities and Politics of Intercultural Penetration and Exchange'. In Patrice Pavis (ed.) *The Intercultural Perfomance Reader*. London: Routledge, pp. 247-256.

Barnes, Clive (1980) '"We Won't Pay" isn't worth it'. *New York Post*, 20 December, p. 15.

Barthes, Roland (1977) *Image, Music, Text*. Trans. Stephen Heath. New York: Hill and Wang.

Bassnett, Susan (1978) 'Translating Spatial Poetry: An Examination of Theatre Texts in Performance'. In James Holmes and José Lambert (eds) *Literature and Translation*. Leuven: ACCO.

____ (1980a) 'An introduction to Theatre Semiotics'. *Theatre Quarterly*, 10.38, 47-53.

____ (1980b) *Translation Studies*. London and New York: Routledge.

____ (1984) 'Towards a Theory of Women's Theatre'. In Herta Schmid and Aloysius Van Kesteren, *Semiotics of Drama and Theatre*. Amsterdam: John Benjamins Publishing Company, pp. 445-467.

____ (1985) 'Ways Through the Labyrinth: Strategies and Methods for Translating Theatre Texts'. In Theo Hermans, *The Manipulation of Literature*. New York: St. Martin Press, pp. 87-103.

____ (1998) 'When a Translation is not a Translation'. In Susan Bassnett and André Lefevere, *Constructing Cultures*. Clevedon: Multilingual Matters, pp. 27-40.

____ (2000) 'Pirandello and Translation'. *Pirandello Studies*, 20, 9-17.

Bassnett, Susan and André Lefevere (eds) (1990) *Translation, History and Culture.* London and New York: Pinter Publishers.

___ (1998) *Constructing Cultures.* Clevedon: Multilingual Matters.

Bassnett, Susan and Trivedi Harish (eds) (1999) *Post Colonial Translation.* London and New York: Routledge.

Bayley, Clare (1991) 'Dead Funny'. *What's On*, 16 January, p. 45.

Behan, Tom (2000a) *Dario Fo Revolutionary Theatre.* London, Pluto Press.

___ (2000b) 'Don's Diary'. *The Times Higher Educational Supplement.* 29 September, p. 8.

Bennett, Susan (1990) *Theatre Audiences A Theory of Production and Reception.* London and New York: Routledge.

Bentley, Eric (1953) *In Search of Theater.* New York: Mentor Books.

___ (ed.) (1964) *The Genius of the Italian Theater.* New York: Mentor Books.

Bentley, Eric and Gerardo Guerrieri (1952) 'Liolà: A country comedy'. In Eric Bentley (ed.) *Naked Masks: Five Plays by Luigi Pirandello.* New York: Dutton.

Billington, Michael (1979) 'Accidental Death of an Anarchist', *Guardian*, 5 October, p. 11.

___ (1980) 'Accidental Death of an Anarchist'. *Guardian*, 7 March, p. 9.

___ (1981) 'Can't Pay? Won't Pay!' *Guardian*, 24 July, p. 13.

___ (1983) 'Can't Pay? Won't Pay!' *Guardian*, 26 February, p. 11.

___ (1984) 'Trumpets and Raspberries'. *Guardian*, 16 November, p. 16.

___ (1990) 'Brecht to the Wall?' *Guardian*, 24 April, p. 11.

___ (1991) 'Farce Forfeit'. *Guardian*, 9 January, p. 38.

___ (1995) 'Bowdlerised Brecht for the bourgeoise'. *Guardian*, 17 November, p. 15

___ (1998) 'The Other Marx brother'. *Guardian*, 10 February, p. 33.

___ (2000) 'Making a living out of war'. *Guardian*, 29 April, p. 29.

Binni, Lanfranco (1975) *Attento te...! Il teatro politico di Dario Fo.* Verona: Bertani.

Blunt Jerry (1967) *Stage Dialects.* Woodstock, The Dramatic Publishing Company.

Bogatyrev, Petr (1971) 'Les signes du theatre'. *Poétique*, 8, 517-530.

Booth, Michael R., Susan Bassnett and John Stoke (1996) *Three tragic actresses: Siddons, Rachel,* Ristori. Cambridge: Cambridge University Press.

Boskin, Joseph (1986) *Sambo: The Rise and Demise of an American Jester.* New York: Oxford University Press.

Bowman, Martin (1998) 'Trainspotting in Montreal: From Scots to Joual'. Unpublished paper presented at the University of East Anglia, Norwich.

Brandt, George W. (1987) 'Six Characters in Bristol'. *The Yearbook of the British Pirandello Society*, 7, 1-10.

Brandt, George W. (1993) *British Television Drama in the 1980s.* Cambridge: Cambridge University Press.

Brecht, Bertolt (1964) *Brecht on Theatre: The Development of an Aesthetics.* Ed. and trans. John Willett. New York: Hill and Wang.

Brisset, Annie (1996) *A Sociocritique of Translation: Theatre and Alterity in Québec, 1968-1988.* Trans. R. Gill and R. Gannon. Toronto: Toronto University Press.

Brook, Peter (1987) *The Shifting Point.* New York: Perennial Library.

Brown, Mark (2003) 'Satire should be ruthless not toothless'. *Scotsman*, 11 May, p. 8.

Bruce Novoa, Juan (1991) 'From Paragonia to Parador: Hollywood's strategy for saving Latin America'. In Juan Villegas and Diana Taylor (eds) *Representations of Otherness in Latin American and Chicano Theater and Film.* Irvine: University of California, pp. 147-159.

Bull, John (1984) *New British Political Dramatists.* London: Macmillan.

Burns, Elizabeth (1972) *Theatricality: A Study of the Conventions in Theatre and Social Life.* London: Longman.

Byrne, Terry (2001) 'First-rate "Johan" is history with a whole new attitude'. *Boston Herald*, 10 September.

Cairns, Christopher (ed.) (1998) *The Commedia dell'arte from the Renaissance to Dario Fo.* Lewiston: Edwin Mellen Press.

___ (2000) *Dario Fo e la "pittura scenica". Arte Teatro Regie 1977-1997.* Napoli: Edizioni Scientifiche Italiane.

Capitta, Gianfranco (2003) 'In scena il re è nudo e l'intelligenza viva'. *Il Manifesto*, 5 December, p. 15.

Capretti, Luciana (1984) 'Fo ironico: "Grazie, Reagan"'. *Il Giorno*, 10 November, p. 31.

___ (1986) 'Mistero Buffo a New York'. *Radio Corriere*, 12 July, pp. 52-3.

Carlson, Marvin (1981) *The Italian Stage: From Goldoni to D'Annunzio.* Jefferson & London: McFarland and Company.

___ (1985a) 'Semiotics and Nonsemiotics in Performance'. *Modern Drama*, 28.4, 670-676.

___ (1985b) 'Theatrical Performance: Illustration, Translation, Fulfilment, or Supplement?' *Theatre Journal*, 37.1, 5-11.

___ (1986) *The Italian Shakespeare: Performances by Ristori, Salvini, and Rossi in England and the United States.* London: Associated University Presses.

___ (1990) *Theatre Semiotics: Signs of Life.* Bloomington: Indiana University Press.

___ (1996) *Performance.* London and New York: Routledge.

Carne, Rosalind (1991) 'Blood Wedding'. *Guardian*, 20 December, p. 19.

Chamberlain, Lori (1988) 'Gender and the Metaphorics of Translation'. *Signs*, 13, 454-472.

Cheshire, D. F. (1974) *Music Hall in Britain.* Newton Abbot: David & Charles.

Christy, Desmond (1985) 'The Worker Knows 300 words'. *Guardian*, 4 April, p. 12.

Clausen Stender, Jørgen (1981) 'Il teatro di Dario Fo in Danimarca'. *Il Veltro*, 25, 385-399.

Clay, Carolyn (1987) 'Fee, Fie, Fo-hum'. *Boston Herald*, 25 June, p. 14.

Clifford, James (1997) *Routes. Travel and Translation in the Late Twentieth Century*. Cambridge: Harvard University Press.

Clurman, Harold (1945) *The Fervent Years: The Story of the Group Theatre and the Thirties*. New York: Hill and Wang.

Colombo, Enzo and Orlando Piraccini (1998) *Pupazzi con rabbia e sentimento*. Milan: Libri Scheiwiller.

Colleran, Jeanne and Jenny Spencer (1998) *Staging Resistance: Essays on Political Theater*. Ann Arbor: The University of Michigan Press.

Connor, John (1984) 'Trumpets and Raspberries'. *City Limits*, 23 November, p. 59.

Coppola, Aniello (1984) 'America in Fo'. *L'unità*, 20 November, p. 34.

Corrigan, Rober W. (ed.) (1965) *Comedy: Meaning and Form*. San Francisco: Chandler Publishing Company.

Corrigan, Rober W. (ed.) (1967) *Masterpiece of the Modern Italian Theatre*. New York: Collier Books.

Cottino-Jones, Marga (1995) Franca Rame on Stage. The Militant Voice of a Resistant Woman. In *Italica,* 72.3, 323-339.

Coveney, Michael (1981) 'Can't Pay? Won't Pay!' *Financial Times*, 24 July, p. 21.

___ (1987) 'Six Characters in Search of an Author'. *Financial Times*, 19 August, p. 13.

___ (1992) 'Much stirring of the melting pot as sparks fly', *Observer*, 18 April, p. 15.

Craig, Sandy (ed.) (1980) *Dreams and Deconstructions*. Ambergate: Amber Lane Press.

D'Aponte, Mimì (1989) 'From Italian Roots to American Relevance: The Remarkable Theatre of Dario Fo'. *Modern Drama*, 32.1, 532-544.

D'Aquino, Niccolò (1984) 'Dario Fo in USA non rinuncia alle sue battute'. *Il Tempo*, 10 November, p. 29.

Da Vinci Nichols, Nina and Jana Bazzoni O'Keefe (1995) *Pirandello & Film*. Lincoln and London: University of Nebraska Press.

Dafoe, Christopher (1980) 'Gripping from the rear'. *The Vancouver Sun*, 13 September, p. 14.

Dall'Osso, Claudia (1984) 'Quarant'anni di teatro su queste tavole di teatro, ma sono ancora giovane, perché ho voglia di gridare'. *Sabato Sera*, 14 January, p. 31.

Davies, Andrew (1987) *Other Theatres*. London: Macmillan.

Davies, Christie (1990) *Ethnic Humor around the* World. Bloomington: Indiana University Press.

Davis, R. G. (1981) 'Dario Fo Off-Broadway: The Making of Left Culture under Adverse Conditions'. *Theatre Quarterly*, 40, 30-36.

___ (1986) 'Seven Anarchists I have Known: American Approaches to Dario Fo'. *New Theatre Quarterly*, 2.8, 313-319.

De Filippo, Eduardo (1956-61) *Cantata dei giorni dispari*, 3 vols. Turin: Einaudi.

___ (1959) *Cantata dei giorni pari*. Turin: Einaudi.

___ (1974) *Saturday, Sunday, Monday: A Play in Three Acts*, English adaptation by Keith Waterhouse and Willis Hall. London: Heinemann Educational Books; New York: Samuel French.

___ (1998) *Filumena*. Trans. Timberlake Wertenbaker. London: Methuen Drama.

de Jongh, Nicholas (1989) 'Sex, lies and Lorca'. *Guardian*, 16 October, p. 22.

de la Tour, Andy (1992) 'Adaptor's Note'. Programme of *The Pope and the Witch*, West Yorkshire Playhouse.

De Marinis, Marco (1982) *Semiotica del teatro*. Milan: Bompiani.

___ (1983) 'Theatrical Comprehension. A Socio-Semiotic Approach'. *Theater*, 12-17.

___ (1987) Dramaturgy of the Spectator. *Tulane Drama Review*, 31.2, 100-114.

Dell, Robert (1960) *The Representation of the Immigrant on the New York stage - 1881 to 1910*, unpublished doctoral dissertation, New York University.

Della Mea, Ivan (1986) 'Prego, non buttate la signora'. *Epoca*, 17 October, pp. 42-43.

Déprats, Jean-Michel (1985) 'Le verbe, instrument du jeu shakespearean'. *Théâtre en Europe*, 7, 70-72.

Derrida, Jacques (1985) 'Des Tours de Babel'. Trans. by Joseph Graham. In Joseph F. Graham (ed.) *Difference in Translation*. Ithaca: Cornell University Press, pp. 165-248.

Di Cenzo, Maria (1996) *The Politics of Alternative Theatre in Britain, 1968-1990. The Case of 7:84*. Cambridge: Cambridge University Press.

Distler, Paul Antoine (1963) *The Rise and Fall of Racial Comics in American Vaudeville*, Doctoral Dissertation, Tulane University.

Dolan, Jill (1988) *The Feminist Spectator as Critic*. Manchester: UMI Research Press.

Donnellan, Declan (1996) 'The Translatable and the Untranslatable. In conversation with David Johnston'. In David Johnston (ed.) *Stages of Translation*. Bath: Absolute Classics, pp. 75-80.

Dort, Bernard (1977) *Theatre en jeu*. Paris: Seuil.

Dovidio, John. F. and John Brigham (1996) 'Stereotyping, Prejudice, and Discrimination: Another Look'. In C. Neil Macrae, Charles Strangor and Miles Hewstone (eds) *Stereotypes and stereotyping*. New York: The Guilford Press, pp. 276-319.

Eco, Umberto (1977) 'Semiotics of Theatrical Performance'. *The Drama Review*, 21, 107-117.

Eddershaw, Margaret (1996) *Performing Brecht. Forty Years of British Performances*. London: Routledge.

Edwardes Jane (1992) 'The Pope and the Witch', *Time Out*, 8-15 April, p. 13.

Elam, Keir (1980) *The Semiotics of Theatre and Drama*. London: Methuen.

Emery, Ed (ed.) (2002) 'Research papers on Dario Fo and Franca Rame'. London: Red Notes.

Ertel, Chris (1989) 'Fine and Foiled Fables'. *The Tab*, 17 October, p. 29.

Esslin, Martin (1973) 'Saturday, Sunday, Monday'. *Plays and Players*, December, p. 42.

Esta, A. J. (1985) 'San Francisco Bay Area'. *Drama Logue*, 31 October - 1 November, p. 10.

Even-Zohar, Itamar (1978) 'The position of translated literature within the literary polysystem'. In James S. Holmes, José Lambert, Raymond van den Broeck (eds) *Literature and Translation*. Louvain: Acco, pp. 117-127.

___ (1979) 'Polysystem Theory, *Poetics Today*, 1.2, Autumn, 237-310.

Even-Zohar, Itamar and Gideon Toury (1981) Translation Theory and Intercultural Relations. Special Issue of *Poetics Today*, 2.4, Summer/Autumn, 9-29.

Fanning, Ursula (1994) 'Six Characters in Search of an Author'. *The Yearbook of the Society for Pirandello Studies*, 14, 72-73.

Farkas, Alessandra (1986) 'Dario Fo and Franca Rame adottati dall'America'. *Corriere della Sera,* 24 June, p. 35.

Farrell, Joseph (1987) 'The Popularity of Dario Fo in Scotland'. *Scottish Theatre News*, 53, 8-10.

___ (1990) 'Adapting *Mistero Buffo* – Author in Search of A Context', *Bulletin of the Society for Italian Studies*, 23, 4-15.

___ (1991) 'Naples, Liverpool and the Vatican: Two British Productions of Fo and De Filippo'. *Bulletin of the Society for Italian Studies*, 24, 25-31.

___ (1995) 'Fo and Feydeau: Is Farce a Laughing Matter?' *Italica*, 72.3, 307-322.

___ (1996) 'Servant of Many Masters'. In David Johnston (ed.) *Stages of Translation*. Bath: Absolute Classics, pp. 45-55.

___ (2000) *Harlequins of the Revolution*. London: Methuen.

Farrell, Joseph and Antonio Scuderi (eds) (2000) *Dario Fo: Stage, Text and Tradition*. Carbondale: Southern Illinois University Press.

Fawcett, Peter and Owen Heathcote (1990) *Translation in Performance: Papers on the Theory and Practice of Translation*. Bradford: University of Bradford.

Felaco, Vittorio (1982) 'Notes on Text and Performance in the Theatre of Dario Fo'. In Michael Herzefeld, Margot D. Lenhart (eds) *Semiotics 1980*. New York: Plenum Press.

Fenton, James (1981) 'Bring on the clowns for the revolution'. *The Sunday Times*, 28 June, p. 38.

Findlay, Bill (1996) 'Talking in Tongues: Scottish Translations 1970-1995'. In Randall Stevenson and Gavin Wallace (eds) *Scottish Theatre Since the Seventies*. Edinburgh: Edinburgh University Press, pp. 186-197.

Fischer-Lichte, Erika (1984) *The Semiotics of Theater*. Bloomington: Indiana University Press.

Fischer-Lichte, Erika, Josephine Riley and Michael Gissenwehrer (eds) (1990) *The Dramatic Touch of Difference: Theatre, Own and Foreign*. Gunter Narr: Verlag Tubingen.

Fish, Stanley (1980) *Is There a Text in This Class? The Authority of Interpretative Communities*. Cambridge, MA: Harvard University Press.

Fitch, Brian T. (1988) *Beckett and Babel: An Investigation into the Status of the Bilingual Work*. Toronto: University of Toronto Press.

Fitzpatrick, Tim and Ksenia Sawczak (1995) 'Accidental Death of a Translator: the difficult case of Dario Fo'. In *About Performance: Working Papers*, 1, Centre for Performance Studies, University of Sydney, pp. 15-34.

Flanagan, Hallie (1940) *Arena: The History of the Federal Theatre*. New York: Benjamin Bloom.

Fleury, Matthew (1985) 'Dario Fo: "L'arte è contaminata. Interview by Matthew Fleury'. *Bomb*, 76-77.

Fo, Dario (1973) 'Morte accidentale di un anarchico'. In Collettivo Teatrale La Comune, *Compagni senza censura*, vol. 2. Milan: Mazzotta Editore, pp. 14-182.

___ (1974) *Morte accidentale di un anarchico*. Turin: Einaudi.

___ (1974-98) *Le commedie di Dario Fo*. Franca Rame (ed.), 13 vols. Turin: Einaudi.

___ (1978) *We Can't Pay? We Won't Pay!* Trans. Lino Pertile, adapt. Robert Walker and Bill Colvill. London: Pluto Press.

___ (1979) 'Accidental Death of an Anarchist'. Trans. Suzanne Cowan. *Theater* (Spring) 10.2, 13-48.

___ (1980) *We Won't Pay! We Won't Pay! A Political Farce*. North American version by R. G. Davis. New York: Samuel French.

___ (1983) 'About Face'. Trans. Dale McAdoo and Charles Mann. *Theater* (Summer/Fall) 14.3, 4-42.

___ (1985a) 'The Open Couple – Very Open'. Trans. Stuart Hood, *Theater*, Winter, 17.1 33-45.

___ (1985b) 'When they beat us, we suffer'. *Index on Censorship*, February, 14.1, p. 59.

___ (1986) 'Ma il giullare non lo fo'. *Il Messaggero*, 12 June, p. 30.

___ (1987a) *Accidental Death*. Trans. Suzanne Cowan, adapt. Richard Nelson. New York: Samuel French.

___ (1987b) 'Almost by chance a Woman: Elizabeth'. Trans. Ron Jenkins. *Theater*, Summmer/Fall, 13.3, 63-97.

___ (1987c) *Archangels Don't Play Pinball*. Trans. R. C. McAvoy and Anna Maria Giugni. London: Methuen.

___ (1989a) *Accidental Death of an Anarchist*. Adapt. Gavin Richards. London: Methuen.

___ (1989b) *About Face*. Trans. Ron Jenkins. New York: Samuel French.

___ (1989c) *Almost by Chance a Woman*. Trans. Ron Jenkins. New York: Samuel French.

___ (1989d) *Archangels Don't Play Pinball*. Trans. Ron Jenkins. New York: Samuel French.

___ (1990a) *Dialogo Provocatorio sul comico, il tragico, la follia e la ragione con Luigi Allegri*. Roma: Laterza.

___ (1990b) 'The Story of the Tiger'. Trans. Ron Jenkins. *Theater*, Winter/Spring, 21.1-2, 38-51.

___ (1991) *Accidental Death of an Anarchist*. Trans. Alan Cumming and Tim Supple. London: Methuen Drama.

___ (1992a) *Plays: One*. Trans. Ed Emery and others. London: Methuen.

___ (1992b) *Johan Padan a la descoverta de le Americhe*. Florence: Giunti.

___ (1992c) *The Pope and the Witch*. Trans. Ed Emery, adapt. Andy de la Tour. London: Methuen.

___ (1994a) *Abducting Diana*. Adapt. Stephen Stenning. London: Oberon Books.

___ (1994b) *Plays: Two*. Trans. Gillian Hanna and others. London: Methuen.

___ (1994c) *The Pope and the Witch. The First Miracle of the Boy Jesus*. Trans. Ed Emery. London: Oberon Books.

___ (1997a) *Manuale minimo dell'attore*. Franca Rame (ed.). Turin: Einaudi.

___ (1997b) *Morte accidentale di un anarchico*. Jennifer Lorch (ed.) Manchester: Manchester University Press.

___ (1997c) *The Pope and the Witch*. Trans. Joan Holden. New York: Samuel French.

___ (1998) *Marino libero! Marino è innocente*. Franca Rame (ed.) Turin: Einaudi.

___ (2000a) 'Sex Don't Mind if I Do!' Trans. Ron Jenkins. In Walter Valeri (ed.), *Franca Rame: A Woman on Stage*.West Lafayette: Bordighera, pp. 63-110.

___ (2000b) *Teatro*. Franca Rame (ed.). Turin: Einaudi.

___ (2001a) *Johan Padan and the Discovery of the Americas*. Trans. Ron Jenkins with the assistance of Stefania Taviano. New York: Grove Press.

___ (2001b) *We Won't Pay! We Won't Pay! and Other Plays*. Franca Rame (ed.) Trans. Ron Jenkins. New York: Theatre Communications Group.

___ (2002) *Il paese dei Mezaràt. I miei primi sette anni (e qualcuno in più)*. Franca Rame (ed.). Milan: Feltrinelli.

___ (2003) *Accidental Death of an Anarchist*. Trans. Simon Nye. London: Methuen.

Fontanella, Luigi (1987) 'Dario Fo e la Rame per dimenticare "L'anarchico"'. *Gazzetta di Parma*, 28 May, p. 28.

Forti, Giovanni (1986) 'Dario Fo a New York diverte gli americani'. *Corriere Aretino dell'Umbria*, 25 May, p. 39.

Foster, Hal (1985) 'For a Concept of the Political in Contemporary Art'. In *Recodings: Art, Spectacle, Cultural Politics*. Port Townsend: Washington: Bay Press, pp. 143-155.

Fowler, Edward (1992) 'Rendering Words, Traversing Cultures: On the Art and Politics of Translating Modern Japanese Fiction'. *Journal of Japanese Studies*, 18, 1-44.

Fox, Sheila (1985) 'The Worker Knows 300 words'. *City Limits*, 29 March, p. 25.

Friedman, Arthur (1989) 'Fo's Fables have humour and charm'. *The Boston Herald*, 7 October, p. 26.

Friedman, Warren A., C. Rossman, D. Sherzer (eds) (1987) *Beckett Translating / Translating Beckett*. University Park: Pennsylvania State University Press.

Gadamer, Hans George (1989) *Truth and Method*, 2nd rev. edn. Trans. rev. Joel Weinsheimer and Donald G. Marshall. New York: Crossroad.

Gale, K. William (1999) 'Trinity to Present Work of a Master Italian Satirist'. *Providence Journal*, 4 April, p. 6.

Galli, Giorgo (1973) 'Chi ha paura di Dario Fo', *Panorama*, 22 November, p. 20.

Gatti, Claudio (1986) 'Io fo l'americano ma ritorno in Italy'. *Europeo*, 12 July, pp. 48-51.

Gilbey, Liz (1991) 'Accidental Death of an Anarchist'. *What's On*, 2 January, p. 45.

Gill, Brendan (1984) 'Accidental Death'. *New Yorker*, 3 December, p. 182.

Gilroy, Harry (1951) 'Mr. Williams Turn to Comedy'. *The New York Times*, 28 January, p. II:1.

Glanville, Brian (1983) 'Master Class from a Master Clown'. *Sunday Times*, 1 May, p. 39.

Godard, Barbara (1995a) 'Theorizing Feminist Discourse/Translation'. In Susan Bassnett and André Lefevere (eds) *Translation, History and Culture*. London: Cassell, pp. 87-97.

____ (1995b) 'A Translator's Diary'. In Sherry Simon (ed.) *Culture in Transit: Translation and the Changing Identities of Quebec Literature*. Montreal: Vehicule Press.

Goffman, Erving (1986) *Frame Analysis*. Boston : Northeastern University Press.

Gómez-Peña, Guillermo (2000) *Dangerous Border Crossers: The Artist Talks Back*. London and New York: Routledge.

Goodman, Walter (1998) 'Interweaving the Real and the Make-Believe'. *The New York Times*, 12 July, p. C27.

Gore-Langton, Robert (1998) 'Pain of a Soul Laid Bare'. *Express*, 19 February, p. 30.

Gorlée, Dinda L. (1994) *Semiotics and the Problems of Translation with Special Reference to the Semiotics of Charles S. Peirce*. Amsterdam: Rodopi.

Gould, Martin (1980) 'We Won't Pay! We Won't Pay!' *Hollywood Reporter*, 19 December, p. 28.

Grassi, Arturo (1973) 'Quel guastafeste di Dario Fo'. *Giornale di Sicilia*, 17 November, p. 15.

Grindrod, Muriel (1964) *Italy*. Oxford: Oxford University Press.

Gross, John (1998) 'Old But Still Smashing'. *Sunday Telegraph*, 11 October, p. 11.

Groppoli, Enrico (2004) 'Il comizio di Fo non è satira ma soltanto noia'. *Il Giornale*, 19 January, p. 26.

____ (1992) 'The Pope and the Witch'. *Sunday Telegraph*, 19 April, p. 15.

Grotowski, Jerzy (1968) *Towards a Poor Theatre*. London: Methuen.

Gussow, Mel (1984a) 'High Placed Hysteria'. *The New York Times*, 13 February, p. C24.

____ (1984b) 'US to give Visa to Fo, Controversial Writer'. *The New York Times*, 31 October, p. C19.

____ (1984c) 'The Case of the Missing Cutting Edge'. *The New York Times*, 25 November, p. II:3.

____ (1986) 'Slaves of Love'. *The New York Times*, 30 May, p. C3.

Hall, Stuart (1991) 'The Local and the Global: Globalization and Ethnicity'. In Anthony D. King (ed.) *Culture, Globalization and the World-System*. London: MacMillan, pp. 19-41.

Hanks, Robert (1995) 'Mother Courage'. *The Independent*, 16 November, p. 15.

Hanna, Gillian (1991) 'Introduction: The Theatre of Dario Fo and Franca Rame'. In Franca Rame and Dario Fo. *A Woman Alone and Other Plays*. Trans. Gillian Hanna, Ed Emery and Christopher Cairns. London: Methuen Drama.

Hare, David (1996) 'Pirandello and Brecht. In Conversation with David Johnston'. In David Johnston (ed.) *Stages of Translation*. Bath: Absolute Classics, pp. 137-143.

Hassan, Ihab and Sally Hassan (eds) (1983) *Innovation/Renovation*. Wisconsin: The University of Wisconsin Press.

Hastings, Michael (1979) 'Glum Theater, or killing them with laughter'. *Plays and Players*, September, p. 12.

Hermans, Theo (ed.) (1985) *The Manipulation of Literature*. London: Croom Helm.

Heylen, Romy (1993) *Translation, Poetics and the Stage: Six French Hamlets*. London and New York: Routledge.

Hilary, Hutcheon (1991) 'Too English by half'. *Tribune*, 11 January, p. 13.

Hiley, Jim (1983) 'Singing of Dark Times'. *The Observer*, 24 April, p. 31.

Hirst, David (1983) 'Pirandello in England: A Question of Style'. *The Yearbook of the British Pirandello Society*, 3, 5-14.

____ (1989) *Dario Fo and Franca Rame*. London: Macmillan.

Holden, Joan (1969) 'Comedy and Revolution'. *Arts in Society*, 6.3, 415-420.

Holderness, Graham (ed.) (1992) *The Politics of Theatre and Drama*. London: Macmillan.

Holland, Peter (1978) 'Brecht, Bond, Gaskill and the Practice of Political Theatre'. *Theatre Quarterly*, 8, p. 24.

Holmes, James and José Lambert (eds) (1978) *Literature and Translation: New Perspectives in Literary Studies*. Leuven: Acco.

Hood, Stuart (1988) 'Open Texts: Some Problems in the Editing and Translating of Dario Fo'. In *The Commedia dell'Arte from the Renaissance to Dario Fo*. Lewiston: Edwin Mellen Press, pp. 336-352.

____ (1991) 'Farce'. Programme of *Sex Please We're Italian*, Young Vic, London.

Hoover, Ted (2004) 'The Accidental Death of an Anarchist'. *The Pittsburgh City Paper*, 17 March, p. 40.

House, Jane and Antonio Attisani (eds) (1995) *Twentieth Century Italian Drama: An Anthology of the First Fifty Years*. New York: Columbia University Press.

Hoyle, Martin (1992) 'Holy Wit'. *Timbe Out*, 8-15 April, pp. 15-16.

____ (1991) 'Accidental Death of an Anarchist'. *The Times*, 13 October, p. 25.

Hunt, Albert (1991) 'Papal Bull', *Plays and Players*, June, pp. 6-7.

Ignatiev, Noel (1995) *How the Irish Became White*. London and New York: Routledge.

Itzin, Catherine (1980) *Stages in the Revolution: Political Theatre in Britain since 1968*. London: Eyre Methuen.

Jenkins, Ron (1994) *Subversive Laughter*. New York: The Free Press.

____ (2000a) 'The Rhythms of Resurrection: Onstage with Fo'. In Joseph Farrell and Antonio Scuderi (eds) *Dario Fo: Stage, Text and Tradition*. Carbondale: Southern Illinois University Press, pp. 30-38.

____ (2000b) 'Translating Tradition: The Theatrical Artistry of Franca Rame'. In *Franca Rame. A Woman on Stage*. West Lafayette: Bordighera, pp. 58-61.

Johnston, David (ed.) (1996) *Stages of Translation*. Bath: Absolute Classics.

____ (2000) 'Theatre as Intercultural Exchange'. In *Reading Across the Lines*. Dublin: The Royal Irish Academy, pp. 11-23.

Kaufman, David (1984) 'The Reactionary Death of An Imported Play'. *Aquarian Weekly*, 19 December, p. 16.

Kaye, Paul (1991) 'Rebirth of an Anarchist'. *London Student*, 10 January, p. 17.

Kelb, Jonathan (1987) 'The Harmless Face of Fo'. *Village Voice*, 22 December, p. 134.

Kershaw, Baz (1992) *The Politics of Performance, Radical Theatre as Cultural Intervention*. London and New York: Routledge.

____ (1996) In Patrick Campbell (ed.) *Analysing performance*. Manchester: Manchester University Press.

Kirby, Michael (1982) 'Nonsemiotic Performance'. *Modern Drama*, 25.1, 105-111.

Kissel, Howard (1984) 'Accidental Death of an Anarchist'. *Women's Wear Daily*, 16 November, p. 18.

Kosow, Dann (1987) 'Farce is stale slapstick'. *What's Up*. June 25 – July 1, p. 25.

Kowzan, Tadeusz (1975) *Littérature et spectacle*. The Hague: Mouton.

Kramar, Silvia (1984) 'Fo? È il sosia di Groucho Marx in mezzo alle luci di Broadway'. *Il Giornale*, 17 November, p. 20.

Kruger, Loren (1992) *The National Stage: Theatre and Cultural Legitimation in England, France and America*. Chicago: The University of Chicago Press.

Lefevere, André (1992a) *Translation, Rewriting and the Manipulation of Literary Fame*. London and New York: Routledge.

____ (1992b) *Translation/History/Culture: A Sourcebook*. London and New York: Routledge.

____ (1998) 'Acculturating Bertolt Brecht'. In Susan Bassnett and André Lefevere *Constructing Cultures*. Clevedon: Multilingual Matters, pp. 109-121.

Liner, Elaine (2004) 'Anarchist. A tour de farce!' *Dallas Morning News*, 13 March, p. 10E.

London, John, 'Theatrical Poison: Translating for the Stage'. In Peter Fawcett and Owen Heathcote (eds) *Translation in Performance*. Bradford: University of Bradford, 1981, pp. 141-167.

Lorch, Jennifer (1983) 'Liolà'. *The Yearbook of the British Pirandello Society*, 3, 100-101.

___ (1991) 'The Rise of the 'Mattatore in Late Nineteenth-Century Italian Theatre'. In J. R. Dashwood and J. E. Everson, *Writers and Performers in Italian Drama from the Time of Dante to Pirandello*. Lewiston: The Edwin Mellen Press, pp. 115-128.

___ (ed.) (1997) *Morte accidentale di un anarchico*. Manchester: Manchester University Press.

___ (2000) *'Morte Accidentale* in English'. In Joseph Farrell & Antonio Scuderi (eds) *Dario Fo: Stage, Text and Tradition*. Carbondale: Southern Illinois University Press, pp. 143-160.

Lowry, Mark (2004a) 'Why this 'Anarchist' has two lives'. *Fort Worth Star Telegram*, 11 January, p. 3D.

___ (2004b) 'Bravo for anarchy at the Dallas Theater Center'. *Star Telegram*, 20 January, p. 8D.

Mackie Diane and David Hamilton (1996) 'Social Psychological Foundations of Stereotype Formation'. In C. Neil Macrae, Charles Strangor and Miles Hewstone, (eds) *Stereotypes and stereotyping*. New York: The Guilford Press, pp. 41-78.

Mander, Raymond and Joe Mitchenson (1965) *British Music Hall*. London: Studio Vista.

Mann, Charles (1980) 'Fo No-Show Doesn't mean No Fo Show'. *Village Voice*, 17-23 December, p. 114.

Marcuson, Lewis (1990) *The Stage Immigrant: The Irish, Italians and Jews in American Drama, 1920-1960*. New York: Garland Publishing.

Martorella, Rosanne (1977) 'The Relationship Between Box Office and Repertoire: A Case Study of Opera'. *Sociological Quarterly*, 18, 354-366.

Marzio, Peter C. (ed.) (1976) *A Nation of Nations*. New York: Harper and Row Publishers.

Mateo, Marta (1995) 'Constraints and Possibilities of Performance Elements in Drama Translations'. *Perspectives, Studies in Translatology*, 3.1, 21-33.

McDonagh, Melanie (1991) 'Accidental Death of an Anarchist'. *Evening Standard*, 8 January, p. 37.

McFerran, Ann (1985) The Worker Knows 300 words. *Time Out*, 28 March, p. 18.

McGrath, John (1981) *A Good Night Out. Popular Theatre: Audience, Class and Form*. London: Eyre Methuen.

___ (1985) 'Popular Theatre and the Changing Perspective of the Eighties. Interview by Tony Mitchell'. *New Theatre Quarterly*, 1.4, 390-399.

McMillan, D. and J. Knowlson (eds) (1993) *The Theatrical Notebooks of Samuel Beckett*. London: Faber and Faber.

McMillan, Joyce (2003). 'Mistero Buffo'. *Scotsman*, 30 April, p. 11.

McNally, William (1919) *McNally's Bulletin: A book of Comedy*, vol. 2. New York: W. McNally.

Mellor, G. J. (1970) *The Northern Musical Hall*. Newcastle: Frank Graham.

Melrose, Susan (1994) *A Semiotiocs of the Dramatic Text*. New York: St Martin's Press.

Mencarelli, Aldo (1984) 'Dario Fo: Usa aspettami, arrivo'. *Paese Sera*, 1 November, p. 27.

Merolla, James A. (1999) 'Cast is the strength of 'We Won't Pay!' *Sun Chronicle*, 17 April, p. 17.

Mignone, Mario (1981) 'Dario Fo: Jester of the Italian Stage'. *Italian Quarterly*, n. 85, 47-56.

___ (ed.) (1988) *Pirandello in America*. Roma: Bulzoni Editore.

Miretti, Stefania (1986) 'Che Mistero Buffo questo successo!' *Stampa Sera*, 30 June, p. 27.

Mitchell, Tony (1989) *File on Dario Fo*. London: Methuen.

___ (1999) *Dario Fo, People's Court Jester* (rev. and exp. edn). London: Routledge.

Morley, Sheridan (1979) 'Full Marx'. *Punch*, 24 October, p. 73.

Munk, Erika (1980) 'Cross Left'. *Village Voice*, 2 June, pp. 86-90.

___ (1984) 'Accident Prone'. *Village* Voice, 27 November, p. 119.

Nadotti, Maria (1986) 'Miss Liberty è nuda', *Noi donne*, September, 60-63.

Nelsen, Don (1981) 'We Won't Pay'. *Daily News*, 8 January, p. 57.

Nightingale, Benedict (1984) 'Sweetener'. *News Statesman*, 23 November, pp. 36-38.

___ (1991) 'Accidental Death of an Anarchist'. *The Times*, 9 January, p. 14.

___ (1995) 'Canny user of mother wit'. *The Times*, 16 November, p. 16.

Nuova Scena (1970) *Compagni senza censura*, vol. 2. Milan, Mazzotta Editore.

Nye, Simon (2003) 'Anarchy in the UK'. *Guardian*, 19 February, p. 25.

O'Connor, John and Lorraine Brown (1980) *Free, Adult Uncensored: The Living History of the Federal Theatre Project*. London: Eyre Methuen.

O'Keefe Bazzoni, Jane (1990) 'Pirandello per il pubblico americano. Traduzioni e riadattamenti dei *Sei personaggi in cerca d'autore'*. *Rivista di Studi Pirandelliani*, 8.5, 59-70.

Orenstein, Claudia (1998) *Festive Revolutions: The politics of Popular Theater and the San Francisco Mime Troupe*. Jackson: University Press of Mississippi.

Pagnini, Marcello (1970) 'Per una semiologia del teatro classico'. *Strumenti Critici*, 12, 121-140.

___ (1980) *Pragmatica della letteratura*. Palermo: Sellerio Editore.

Parini, Sergio (1984) 'Fo l'America e ritorno'. *Il Manifesto*, 20 November, p. 25.

Pascoli, Giovanni and Massimo Venturi (1985) 'Chi ha paura di Dario Fo'. *Jonas*, May, p. 34.

Pavis, Patrice (1982) *Languages of the Stage*. New York: Performing Arts Journal Publications.

___ (1992) *Theatre at the Crossroads of Culture*. Trans. Loren Kruger. London and New York: Routledge.

___ (1996) *The Intercultural Performance Reader*. London and New York: Routledge.

Paz, Octavio (1992) 'Translation, Literature and Letters'. Trans. Irene del Corral. In Rainer Schulte and John Biguenet (eds) *Theories of Translation: An Anthology of Essays from Dryden to Derrida.* Chicago: Chicago University Press, pp. 152-163.

Peachment, Chris (1987) 'In Search of a Stage'. *The Times*, 18 March, p. 15.

Pirandello, Luigi (1922) *Three Plays.* Trans. Arthur Livingston and Edward Storer. New York: Dutton.

_____ (1928) *The One-Act-Plays of Luigi* Pirandello. Trans. Elisabeth Abbott, Arthur Livingston and Blanche Valentine Mitchell. New York: Dutton.

_____ (1931) *As You Desire Me.* Trans. Samuel Putnam. New York: Dutton.

_____ (1932) *Tonight We Improvise.* Trans. Samuel Putnam. New York: Dutton.

_____ (1950) *Diana and Tuda.* Trans. Marta Abba. London: Samuel French.

_____ (1952) *Naked Masks.* Eric Bentley (ed.) Trans. Edward Storer and others. New York: Dutton.

_____ (1954) *Six Characters in Search of an Author.* Trans. Frederick May. London: Heinemann.

_____ (1958a) *Maschere Nude.* 2 vols. Milan: Arnoldo Mondadori Editore.

_____ (1958b) *The Mountain Giants and Other Plays.* Trans. Marta Abba. New York: Crown Publisher.

_____ (1959a) *The Man with the Flower in his Mouth.* Trans. Frederick May. Leeds: The Pirandello Society.

_____ (1959b) *The Rules of the Game and Two Other Plays.* E. Martin Browne (ed.) Trans. Robert Rietty and Frederick May. Harmondsworth: Penguin Books.

_____ (1962) *To Clothe The Naked and Two Other* Plays. Trans. William Murray. New York: Dutton.

_____ (1973) 'Illustratori, attori e traduttori'. In *Saggi, poesie e scritti vari.* Milan: Mondadori, pp. 207-224.

_____ (1979) *Six Characters in Search of an Author.* Trans. John Linstrum. London: Methuen Drama.

_____ (1985) *Three Plays.* John Linstrum (ed.). Trans. Robert Rietty and others. London: Methuen.

_____ (1988) *Luigi Pirandello: Collected Plays,* vol. 2, Robert Rietty (ed.). Trans. Felicity Firth, Henry Reed and Diane Cilento. London: John Calder; New York: Riverrun Press.

_____ (1990) *The Mountain Giants.* Trans. Felicity Firth. *The Yearbook of the British Pirandello Society,* 10.

_____ (1992) *Luigi Pirandello: Collected Plays,* 3 vols, Robert Rietty (ed.). Trans. Robert Rietty and others. London: John Calder; New York: Riverrun Press.

_____ (1993) 'Sei personaggi in cerca d'autore'. In Alessandro d'Amico (ed.) *Maschere Nude,* vol. 2. Milan: Arnoldo Mondadori Editore.

_____ (1998a) *Naked.* Trans. Nicholas Wright. London: Nick Hern Books.

_____ (1998b) *Six Characters in Search of an Author,* in a new adaptation by Robert Brustein and the American Repertory Theatre Company. Chicago: Ivan R. Dee.

Piscator, Edward (1980) *The Political Theatre*. Trans. H. Rorrison. London: Methuen.

Poyatos, Fernando (1982) 'Nonverbal Communication in the Theatre: The Playwright/Actor/Spectator-Relationship'. In Ernest W. B. Hess-Luttich (ed.) *Multimedial Communication 2: Theatre Semiotics*. Tubingen: Gunter Narr Verlag, pp. 75-94.

Provvedini, Claudia (1984) 'Alla scoperta dell'America', *Il Tirreno*, 8 November, p. 31.

Puppa, Paolo (1978) *Il teatro di Fo. Dalla scena alla piazza*. Venezia: Marsilio.

____ (1987) *Dalle parti di Pirandello*. Roma: Bulzoni Editore.

____ (2000) 'Tradition, Traditions and Dario Fo'. Trans. Joseph Farrell. In Joseph Farrell and Antonio Scuderi (eds) *Dario Fo: Stage, Text and Tradition*.

Radin, Victoria (1980) 'Why has the Fringe Gone West'. *The Observer*, 2 March, p. 36.

Rame, Franca (1994) 'Introduction'. In Dario Fo, Dario *Plays*, vol. 2. London: Methuen Drama.

Rame, Franca and Dario Fo (1981) *Female Parts*. Trans. Margaret Kunzle, adapt. Olwen Wymark. London: Pluto Press.

____ (1991) *A Woman Alone and Other Plays*. Trans. Gillian Hanna, Ed Emery and Christopher Cairns. London: Methuen Drama.

____ (2004) 'I am Ready. Interview by Stefania Taviano'. *The Open Page*, n. 9, March 2004, 19-23.

Reinelt, Janelle (1998) 'Notes for a Radical Democratic Theater: Productive Crises and the Challenge of Indeterminacy'. In Jeanne Colleran and Jenny S. Spencer (eds) *Staging Resistance. Essays on Political Theater*. Ann Arbor: University of Michigan Press, pp. 283-300.

Rich, Frank (1984) 'The Theater: Dario Fo, "Death of an Anarchist" Farce Opens at Belasco'. *The New York Times,* 16 November, p. C3.

Robinson, Douglas (1991) *The Translator's Turn*. Baltimore: John Hopkins University Press.

Romy, Heylen (1993) *Translation, Poetics and the Stage: Six French Hamlets*. London and New York: Routledge.

Roorbach, Orville Augustus (1969) *Minstrel Gags and End Men's Handbook*. Upper Saddle River, NJ: Literature House.

Ruffini, Franco (1978) *Semiotica del testo. L'esempio teatro*. Roma: Bulzoni Editore.

____ (1985) 'Testo/scena: drammaturgia dello spettacolo e dello spettatore'. *Versus*, 41, 21-40.

Rutherford, Malcolm (1992) 'The Pope and the Witch'. *Financial Times*, 15 April, p. 21.

Salomon, Alisa (1983a) 'Reviews of *About Face* and *No Se Paga!*'. *Performing Arts Journal*, 7.2, 63-66.

____ (1983b) 'Zoo Story'. *Village Voice*, 2 August, p. 35.

____ (1984) 'Broadway's Fo'. *Village Voice*, 27 November, p. 119.

Samuel, Raphael, Ewan MacColl and Stuart Cosgrove (1985) *Theatres of the left 1880-1935. Workers Theatre Movements in Britain and America.* London: Routledge and Kegan Paul.

Schechter, Joel (1984) 'The un-American Satire of Dario Fo'. *Partisan Review,* 1, 112-119.

Scolnicov, Hanna and Peter Holland (eds) (1989) *The Play Out of Context: Transferring plays from Culture to Culture.* Cambridge: Cambridge University Press.

Scuderi, Antonio (1998) *Dario Fo and Popular Performance.* New York, Legas.

Serpieri, Alessandro (1978) *Come comunica il teatro: dal testo alla scena.* Milan: Il Formichiere.

Shank, Theodore (1982) *American Alternative Theatre.* London: MacMillan.

Sierz, Alek (1997) 'British Theatre in the 1990s: a brief political economy'. *Media, Culture and Society,* 19.3, 461-469.

Simon John (1980) 'Maternal Tiger, Libidinous Mice', *New York,* 25 February, p. 64.

Simon, Sherry (1988) 'Out from Undercover'. In David Homel and Sherry Simon (eds) *Mapping Literature: the Art and Politics of Translation.* Montréal: Véhicule Press, pp. 51-54.

_____ (1996) *Gender in Translation: Cultural Identity and the Politics of Transmission.* London and New York: Routledge.

Snyder, Robert W. (1989) *The Voice of the City: Vaudeville and Popular Culture in New York.* New York and Oxford: Oxford University Press.

Spencer, Charles (1992) 'A Nasty Habit'. *Daily Telegraph,* 15 April, p. 17.

_____ (1995) 'Boring old Brecht is brought to life by stunning Rigg'. *Daily Telegraph,* 15 November, p. 19.

Stasio, Marilyn (1987) Dario Fo takes on Italy. *New York Post,* December 1, p. 20.

States, Bert O. (1985) *Great Reckonings in Little Rooms: On the Phenomenology of Theatre.* Berkeley: University of California Press.

Strangor, Charles and Mark Schaller (1996). 'Stereotypes as Individual and Collective Representations'. In C. Neil Macrae, Charles Strangor and Miles Hewstone (eds) *Stereotypes and Stereotyping.* New York: The Guilford Press, pp. 3-37.

Stuart, Jan (1983) 'The Oldest Profession: Estelle Parsons and the Business of Acting'. *New York Native,* August - September, p. 50.

Stutzin, Leo (1981) 'About Face sparkles with laughter'. *The Modesto Bee,* 17 October, p. 15.

Sypher, Wylie (1956) *Comedy.* Garden City: Doubleday.

Taylor, Paul (1991) 'A cold, wet marriage'. *Independent,* 19 December, p. 18.

Taviano, Stefania (2000) 'British Acculturation of Italian Theatre'. In Andrew Chesterman, Natividad Gallardo, Yves Gambier (eds). *Translation in Context.* Amsterdam, Philadelphia: J. Benjamins, pp. 339-352.

___ (2001) 'Dario Fo and Franca Rame in the UK'. In Edward M. Batley and David Bradby (eds) *Morality and Justice - The Challenge of European Theatre*. Amsterdam, Rodopi, pp. 285-298.

Taviano, Stefania and Jennifer Lorch (2000) 'Producing Pirandello in England'. *Pirandello Studies*, 20, 18-30.

Thomson, Peter and Glendyr Sacks (eds) (1994) *The Cambridge Companion to Brecht*. Cambridge: Cambridge University Press.

Tisdall, Caroline (1980) 'The collective explosion'. *Guardian*, 1 March, p. 9.

Toll, Robert C. (1974) *Blacking Up*. New York: Oxford University Press.

Tornqvist, Egil (1991) *Transposing Drama*. London: MacMillan.

Townsend, Charles (1969) *Negro* Minstrels. Upper Saddle River, NJ: Literature House.

Treglown, Jeremy (1980) 'The Ethics of Translation'. *Times Literary Supplement*, 22 August, p. 25.

Trincia, Stefano (1984) 'Grazie a Reagan, eccoci a Broadway'. *Il Messaggero*, 10 November, p. 33.

Ubersfeld, Anne (1978) *Lire le theatre*. Paris: Éditions Sociales.

___ (1981) *L'école du spectateur*. Paris: Messidor.

___ (1982) 'The Pleasure of the Spectator'. *Modern Drama*, 25.1, 127-139.

Valentini, Chiara (1973) 'Pum Pum! Il questore'. *Panorama*, 22 November, pp. 58-59.

___ (1977) *La storia di Fo*. Milan: Feltrinelli.

Van Erven Eugène (1988) *Radical People's Theatre*. Bloomington: Indiana University Press.

Vanderauwera, Ria (1985) *Dutch Novels Translated Into English*. Amsterdam: Rodopi.

Veltrusky, Jiři (1977) *Drama as Literature*. Lisse: The Peter de Ridder Press.

Venuti, Lawrence (1995) *The Translator's Invisibility*. London and New York: Routledge.

___ (1998) *The Scandals of Translation*. London and New York: Routledge.

Viagas, Robert (1983) 'Face: Mirror of a frazzled mind', *Fairpress*, April 13, p. C2.

Vicentini, Claudio (1993) *Pirandello: Il disagio del teatro*. Venezia: Marsilio.

Vitez, Antoine (1996) *Le devoir de traduire*. Montpellier: Editions Climats & Maison Antoine Vitez.

Volli, Ugo (1976) 'La droga? Un problema politico'. *La Repubblica*, 4 March, p. 20.

Walsh, Martin W. (1985) 'The Proletarian Carnival of Fo's *Non si Paga! Non si Paga!*'. *Modern Drama*, 28.2, 211-222.

Wandor, Micheline (1980) 'The personal is Political'. In Sandy Craig, *Dreams and Deconstruction, Alternative Theatre in Britain*. Ambergate: Amber Lane Press, pp. 49-58.

Wardle, Irving (1981) 'Woman's dramatic predicament'. *The Times*, 29 June, p. 6.

___ (1984) 'Hooters, Trumpets and Raspberries'. *The Times*, 5 January, p. 13.

Warren Friedman A., C. Rossman and D. Sherzer (eds) (1987) *Beckett Translating/Translating Beckett*. University Park: Pennsylvania State University Press.

Warren, Robert (1980) 'Bella Napoli', *New Yorker,* February, p. 99.

Weiner, Bernard (1979) 'Mime Troupe Breaks with Tradition, Goes Indoors with We Can't Pay'. *San Francisco Sunday Examiner and Chronicle*, 9 December, pp. 22-23.

___ (1985) 'Eureka' Italian Loony 'Lucy' Farce – With a Twist'. *San Francisco Chronicle*, October 31, p. 74.

West, Julian (1987) 'Dario Fo's "Pinball" only at times lights up spectacularly'. *The Tech*, June 23, p. 7.

Wilson, Edwin (1984) 'America, At Last, Welcomes Dario Fo'. *Wall Street Journal*, November 20, p. 28.

Wing, Joylynn (1990) 'The Performance of Power and the Power of Performance: Rewriting the Police State in Dario Fo's *Accidental Death of an Anarchist'*. *Modern Drama*, 23, 139-149.

Wittke, Carl (1952) 'The Immigrant Theme on the American Stage'. *The Mississipi Valley Historical Review*, 39.2, September, 211-232.

Wood, Sharon (1991) 'Enrico Four'. *The Yearbook of the Society for Pirandello Studies*, 11, 94-95.

Woodrough, Elizabeth (1995) *Women in European Theatre*. London: Intellect.

Worth, Katherine (1987) 'Six Characters at the National Theatre (2)'. *The Yearbook of the British Pirandello Society*, 7, 36-43.

Worthen, W. B. (1995) 'Homeless Words: Field Day and the Politics of Translation.' *Modern Drama*, 38.1, 22-41.

Wyer, S. Robert Jr. (1998) *Stereotype Activation and Inhibition*. Mahwak, NJ: L. Erlbaum Associates Publishers.

Young, B. A. (1965) 'Mother Courage'. *Financial Times*, 13 May, p. 29.

Ziv, Avner (ed.) (1988) *National Styles of Humor*. New York: Greenwood Press.

Zuber, Ortrun (ed.) (1980) *Languages of the Theatre: Problems in the Translation and the Transposition of Drama*. Oxford: Pergamon.

Index